FOOTBALL'S RIVALS FOREVER

30 OLDEST AND FIERCEST SOCCER DERBIES

IN THE WORLD

SHANTANU GUPTA

"It is always possible to bind together a considerable number of people in love, so long as there are other people left over to receive the manifestations of their aggressiveness."

- Sigmund Freud (Civilization and Its Discontents, Published in 1930)

Contents

INTRODUCTION

The famous Prussian general and military strategist Carl von Clausewitz once said that politics is the continuation of war by other means.

Had he lived long enough, he may well have been tempted to update his aphorism, substituting the word 'football' for 'politics'.

Certainly the rivalries that have developed between certain teams throughout the years come close, and, on occasion, cross the line between acute tension and armed conflict. And, the root cause of such rivalries, often go way beyond sporting differences, embracing wider elements drawn from a divergence of economic, social, political and religious views and attitudes.

People tend to follow the football club that their parents and grandparents before them supported. It is something inherited in the genes, passed down from generation to generation. .

Nowadays, in some countries, away fans are banned in a bid to cut down on the violence, but that does not stop legions of riots with police equipped with riot shields and batons having to be deployed in the streets to try and keep order on derby day.

And because many of the fans live in the same city and attend the same school or office, they still have to live with each other for the rest of the time.

So prevalent are these derbies and rivalries throughout club football, irrespective of country or region, that in compiling a list of the fiercest, the hardest decision was which ones to leave out.

What follows, therefore, is just a sample of some of the best-known elements of what is a much bigger picture.

THE A23 DERBY

CRYSTAL PALACE V BRIGHTON & HOVE ALBION

Location: Southern England

First Meeting: 25 December 1920

Whilst some rivalries owe their origin to clear economic, social, political or religious differences between two clubs, often in the same city or close geographical proximity to each other, there are other derbies that, from the outside, appear to have no logic behind them.

Crystal Palace and Brighton & Hove Albion falls into the latter category.

45 miles separate the two clubs, and it is often referred to as the A23 derby because of the major trunk road running between them.

Although, they are both part of the Premier League in the 2022-23 season, that was not always the case and, at one stage, they were not often in the same league together. And, when they did meet, there used to be very little overt hostility between players and fans.

Today, though, it is these two meetings that supporters of both clubs eagerly look up in the fixtures list at the start of a season, and the ones that they want to win above all other.

The origins of the rivalry

For many years matches between the two were regarded as run of the mill fixtures, nothing to make them stand out.

However, by the early 1970s, there were simmers of discontent, and, although they were both languishing in Division Three at the time, clashes between fans were not uncommon.

However, it all spilled over into downright acrimony in 1976. At the time, Palace were managed by Terry Venables, and Brighton by Alan Mullery, two men who, although they had both been team-mates at Tottenham Hotspur together during their playing days, did not get along.

The two men were relatively young, dynamic and the source of good copy for the newspapers at the time.

The pair were both chasing promotion that year, Brighton finished second and Palace third, and they were also both drawn together in the first round of the FA Cup.

With the first match and then the subsequent replay ending in a draw, a second replay to decide the tie was held, with Chelsea's Stamford Bridge stadium chosen as the venue.

Palace won the game by a single goal, but Mullery was incensed because he felt the referee Ron Challis had disallowed a perfectly good equaliser for his side. He was furious and went to confront Challis at the final whistle. As he walked back down the tunnel, Palace fans spat at him, prompting Mullery to flick V-signs at them.

Mullery then gave an incendiary post-match interview, in which he laid into the Palace supporters and then belittled the Palace players, saying that he would not give a "fiver" for any of them. To make his point he produced five £1 notes from his pocket, ripped them up, and threw them on the floor.

In the mayhem that followed, boiling coffee was poured over Mullery.

Meanwhile referee Challis (who was promptly nicknamed "Challis of Palace") needed police protection, first to protect him from Mullery, and then later as he tried to leave Stamford Bridge surrounded by a mob of angry Brighton fans.

Venables left Palace in 1980, and Mullery Brighton a year later, but a relatively short interlude had left a lasting legacy in the history of both clubs.

Ironically, Mullery became Palace manager in 1982, but it was not a happy experience for him or the club. He was subject to constant abuse, and threats turned to violence after a particularly humiliating home defeat as he was ambushed by a group of Palace fans on the way back to his car. A friend rescued him, but he was left badly scarred after the incident.

There is also an element of snobbism to the rivalry now. Both have seen their share of problems off the field. Palace have twice been in administration, whilst in 1996 Brighton came within one game of being relegated from the football league itself.

At that time, Brighton's home for 95 years, the Goldstone Ground, had been sold from under them to property developers, and, although they survived, they endured a nomadic existence after that, with home games played for a while at the Withdean Stadium and then Gillingham's Priestfield Stadium, necessitating a 150 mile round trip for anybody wanting to watch a home game.

However, when they moved into the purpose built state of the art Amex Stadium, more fuel was added to the rivalry, with Palace accusing Brighton of being nouveau riche. Whilst Palace continues to call Selhurst Park home, it is one of the older football league grounds and in need of modernisation.

Some Palace die-hards maintain that many Brighton fans were formerly Manchester United supporters and only switched allegiance when they had a decent home stadium of their own.

Notable incidents

In 1985 the Brighton fans were left incensed by a tackle on their popular Irish winger Gerry Ryan by Palace's Henry Hughton that broke his leg in three places. In fact, they were both team-mates together for the Republic of Ireland and Ryan felt no lasting animosity to Hughton. But the incident sparked sustained crowd violence after the game and in the surrounding streets.

In 1989, there was a game between the two teams that featured five penalties, four of them awarded to Crystal Palace. They contrived to miss three of them, but still ended up winning the game.

In the 2012 – 2013 season, they met on four occasions and then once again in a two-legged promotion play-off. After the first match at Selhurst Park ended in a goalless draw, Palace travelled to Brighton for the away leg, only to find human faeces smeared all over their changing room. It was later blamed on the Brighton coach driver.

In a classic case of mistaken identity, a Palace player later admitted it was their own coach driver who was responsible, in a bid to put Brighton in a bad light!

Meanwhile, fan violence is common. When a 12 foot fence was erected outside Selhurst Park to separate fans, fighting instead broke out at nearby Selhurst and Norwood Junction stations. Bricks have been thrown at Palace fans as they have been escorted to the Amex Stadium by the police, and trains from South London carrying Palace supporters no longer stop in Brighton on derby day.

Most famous matches

It was the FA Cup replay back in 1976 that is widely blamed for starting the rivalry in the first place. There are other matches too that fuelled the rivalry to what it is today

In 1989 referee Kelvin Morton awarded five penalties in the game between the two at Selhurst Park in 27 minutes, a Football League record. Palace missed three of the four awarded to them but still the home side went on to win 2 – 1.

History was made when the two teams were drawn against each other for a third round tie in the FA Cup in January 2018, because it was the first match in England to use VAR (Video Assisted Referee).

And there was another first in the match at Brighton the following season, when Brighton became the first team in Premier League history to have two substitutes score for them before half-time.

Crossing the divide

Apart from *Alan Mullery* who managed both clubs, perhaps the player most associated with both clubs in recent memory is striker *Glenn Murray*.

He had an itinerant career which saw him play in the top six tiers of English football, and he had a spell in North America as well. He first joined Brighton from Rochdale in 2008, and helped them win promotion from League One with 22 goals.

Murray became a fan favourite with the Seagulls, but in 2011 he crossed the divide and made the move to Palace, where he enjoyed even more success, and helped them win promotion back to the Premier League. He scored 30 goals in their promotion season, an EFL Championship record that stood until recently.

He returned to Brighton in 2016, and his goals helped them reach the Premier League for the first time in their history. Murray is Brighton's second highest ever goalscorer, and is in the top 30 for Crystal Palace.

Interesting facts about the rivalry

- Some believe that Palace fans manufactured the rivalry because they were afraid of taking on local rivals Millwall, who had a fearsome reputation at the time (and still do!)
- Crystal Palace were originally nicknamed "the Glaziers", and were only rebranded as "The Eagles" in 1973. One version of the Brighton nickname "The Seagulls" is because seagulls cr*p on Eagles (on the other hand eagles have been known to eat seagulls!).
- The rivalry is sometimes erroneously called the M23 derby because of the motorway between South London and Sussex. In truth, the M23 does not start or finish near either ground.

The Ruhr Derby

Borussia Dortmund v Schalke 04

Location: North Rhine-Westphalia, Germany

First Meeting: 3 May 1925

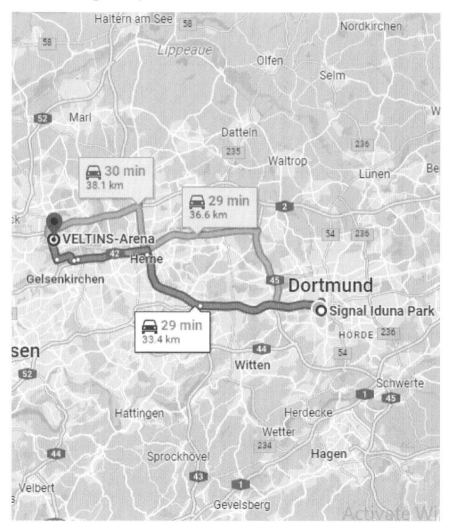

Although Germany has many footballing rivalries, that between Dortmund and Schalke transcends all of them, and is regarded as one of the fiercest in world football.

Yet, whilst economic, religious or political differences lie at the heart of many other rivalries, the cities of Dortmund and Gelsenkirchen (the home of Schalke), have more in common than what divides them as they are situated just 20 miles apart.

Both are industrial cities in the heart of what used to be the centre of German coal and steel production, and the two clubs still have a predominantly working-class fan base.

For all that, there is no middle ground for local football fans, who are either Dortmund or Schalke supporters. It is a region that values hard work, dedication and loyalty more than anything, and supporters of these two clubs expect these values to be encapsulated in the players that pull on their respective shirts.

The most ardent among those fans will even refuse to say the name of the other team out loud in public – Schalke are known as "Herne West" whilst in equally disparaging tones, Dortmund are referred to as "Ludenscheid Nord."

The origins of the rivalry

Schalke were formed in 1904 and Dortmund five years later, but, in the early years, they both played in local leagues, and it was only in the 1924/25 season that the two had their first competitive meeting.

Schalke were very much the dominant club, not only in the Ruhr region, but in Germany, winning six German championships between 1934 and 1942, inspired by the legendary Ernst Kuzorra and playing a brand of one touch football similar to "tiki-taka".

It would be 18 years before Dortmund won their first derby, but the tide gradually began to turn, and they became the dominant force in Western Germany.

When the Bundesliga was formed in 1963, they both were founding members, but it has been Dortmund who have enjoyed far more success since then, winning five league titles to none for their rivals, and also winning the Champions League in 1997.

Despite the comparative differences in fortunes in the past sixty years, the rivalry remains as intense as ever, and winning a derby means more to fans of both clubs than any other result in the season.

Noticeable incidents

It is inconceivable now, but when Schalke won their first national title in 1934 away against Nuremberg in Berlin, the train carrying the Schalke players was stopped and celebrated at the Dortmund station, and the squad was escorted to the town hall to sign the visitors' book.

At a Ruhr derby in 1969, a German shepherd dog Rex took a bite out of Schalke player Freidel Rausch's behind, and team-mate Gerd Neuser was bitten on the thigh. Rausch was able to carry on after getting vaccinated for rabies by the team doctor, but had to sleep on his stomach for two nights, and still bore the scar several years later.

In retaliation for Rex's actions, in the return fixture, Schalke unveiled their new mascots, when their president Guenter Siebert borrowed several lions for the day from a local zoo, and paraded it around the pitch before kick-off.

Even though the 2007 – 2008 season was largely a disappointing one for Dortmund, they did have the satisfaction of beating Schalke in the penultimate match of the season, effectively denying them, the title. The following weekend a group of Dortmund fans commissioned a plane to fly a banner which said "ein leben lang keine schale in der hand" (a lifetime without your hands on the trophy).

Most famous matches

Schalke 1 – 2 Dortmund (May, 2005)

Coming into this match Dortmund had failed to beat Schalke in 12 previous meetings stretching back over more six years. But they took the lead twice and an inspired performance by goalkeeper Roman Weidenfeller helped them end their long hoodoo.

Dortmund 2 – 0 Schalke (May, 2007)

Heading into the penultimate weekend of the season, Schalke were chasing their first Bundesliga title since 1958, and were leading the table by one point. But a two nil loss to their great rivals enabled Stuttgart to overtake them and win the Bundesliga on the last day of the season.

Dortmund 3 - 3 Schalke (September, 2008)

Jurgen Klopp's first derby in charge of Dortmund was a fiery affair with a lot of drama. Dortmund went three goals down early in the second-half. They pulled two goals back, Schalke had two men sent off inside three minutes, and Dortmund equalised with a last minute penalty.

Dortmund 4 – 4 Schalke (November, 2017)

Schalke fans in the stadium and at home watched in horror as their side trailed by four goals inside 25 minutes at the home of their great rivals. Schalke coach Domenico Todesco used all three of his substitutes by half-time, and his side came storming back in the second-half to grab an unlikely point. It was only the second time that a team had come from 4 – 0 down in Bundesliga history to claim a result.

Crossing the divide

Given the intense nature of the rivalry, there have been relatively few players that have switched allegiance. However, those have done so successfully include:

Reinhard Libuda

Winger Libuda was a Schalke fan and would go on to play for his boyhood club between 1961 and 1965. Yet the most important goal he scored in his career was for Dortmund in 1966, when he scored the winner in the 1966 European Cup Winners Cup final, becoming the first German side to lift a European trophy.

Ingo Anderbrugge

Anderbrugge made his Dortmund debut aged 20 and spent four seasons with them, before making the short trip to Gelsenkirchen, where he was to remain for 11 years. The midfielder was later voted into Schalke's team of the century, and helped them win the UEFA Cup in 1997.

Andreas Möller

Möller become a Dortmund icon in the mid-1990s, helping them win two Bundesliga titles and the Champions League. His decision, therefore, to then join Schalke sent shock waves throughout the Ruhr region, and many Schalke fans refused to welcome him. Still, he was the driving force in the side that almost won the Bundesliga the following season.

Jens Lehmann

Before the goalkeeper moved to England and joined Arsenal, he had already played for the two great rivals. He had earned legendary status at Schalke where he became the first goalkeeper in the Bundesliga era to score from a corner, and, then, after a brief spell in Italy with AC Milan, moved to Dortmund, helping them win the league title in the 2001/2002 season.

Steffen Freund

Another man whose career took him to North London, Freund was no stranger to breaking taboos. Following reunification, he was one of the first players from East Germany to join a West German club when he moved to Schalke in 1991. And then, two years later, he crossed another divide and moved to Dortmund where he was to win two Bundesliga titles, and the Champions League.

Interesting facts about the rivalry

- The match is sometimes known as the Revierderby, although, strictly speaking, this is a generic term for any match between two clubs based in the Ruhr region of Germany. In reality due to the "Kohlenpott" rule, these other games are given another epithet, such as minor Ruhr derby.
- The first goal ever scored by a goalkeeper in the Bundesliga occurred in a derby match, when Jens Lehmann of Schalke went up for a corner in the dying minutes and headed home.
- The game between the two has finished scoreless nine times – no other Bundesliga fixture has ended in a no-score draw more often.
- Despite that, matches between the two over the years have averaged more than three goals a game.

THE NORTH LONDON DERBY

ARSENAL V TOTTENHAM HOTSPUR

Location: North London, England

First Meeting: 4 December 1909

Although it may look like a homogenous whole to outsiders, London is actually made up of a large number of smaller communities, all of which have their own separate identities. There are broader divisions – East versus West, and North, as opposed to South of the River – but nearly each part of the capital was once a village or parish, who would have treated neighbours with suspicion and sometimes downright antipathy.

The numerous London derbies of today are a projection in many cases of these long standing rivalries. None is more fiercely contested than the North London derby between Arsenal and Tottenham Hotspur – more commonly known as Spurs.

Families and friends may number both Arsenal and Spurs fans among their number, but come derby day and in the weeks before and after it, there is often no love lost.

The origins of the rivalry

Although the two clubs were formed four years apart, Spurs in 1882 and Arsenal in 1886, for the first period of their mutual existence there was no particularly rivalry between the two clubs.

Spurs were formed by a group of schoolboys, and, although they later turned professional, they played in the Southern League and were not admitted to the Football League until 1908.

Arsenal, meanwhile, were not even a North London club initially. They were formed by munitions workers in Woolwich, and initially played their home matches in Plumstead Common in South-East London. Initially known as Dial Square, that became Woolwich Arsenal, and then just Arsenal.

They became the first club from the South of England to join the Football League in 1893, but they struggled because of financial difficulties among munition workers and the rise of more accessible clubs in the capital led to falling attendances.

The club was close to bankruptcy when, in 1913, their Plumstead Stadium grandstand was burnt down by militant suffragettes. To rescue the club's fortunes, businessmen Henry Norris and William Hall decided to move the club north of the river to their new home in Highbury.

Suddenly, Tottenham who had been the only major club in North London, had new neighbours.

However, it was what happened in 1919 that was to trigger the bitter rivalry that exists to this day.

When the league had been suspended due to the First World War hostilities, following the end of the 1914/15 season, Chelsea and Tottenham had occupied the bottom two spots in the table and were relegated. Arsenal, meanwhile, had finished sixth in Second Division.

After the War it was decided to expand the league from 20 to 22 teams, but there were some disputes regarding who would be included in the newly constituted league. Chelsea earned a reprieve but Arsenal, due to intense lobbying by Norris, who was a member of parliament and particularly well connected, got majority of the votes cast, and were elevated at the expense of their rivals.

Even a century after it happened, the injustice still rankles with some Tottenham fans.

Notable Incidents

There have been numerous red cards and fights over the years, with the clash in November 1999 a particular example, with both Freddie Ljungberg and Martin Keown seeing red for the visiting Gooners with the final score 2 – 1 at the White Hart Lane.

And, in more liberal refereeing times, the game in 1975 on the same ground saw all 20 out-field players engage in a mass brawl after one unsavoury tackle.

In 2002, Thierry Henry scored a solo goal from deep inside his own half against Spurs, and his iconic celebration afterwards is now captured in bronze in the statue that honours him outside the Emirates Stadium.

Danish forward Nicklas Bendtner famously dubbed himself the "greatest striker that ever lived" He did little in his career to justify that decision but made himself an instant Gunners hero in 2007 when he scored with his first touch after coming on as a substitute 6 seconds earlier. It remains the fastest goal scored by a substitute in the history of the Premier League.

The following year Arsenal were leading the league match between the two by 4 – 2 with just a minute left on the clock, but two late goals gave Tottenham an unexpected point.

Famous Matches

Tottenham 0 – 1 Arsenal (May, 1971)

The Gunners came to White Hart Lane needing a scoreless draw or win to claim the league title from Leeds United. An 88th minute winner from Ray Kennedy won it for them.

Tottenham 1 – 2 Arsenal (March, 1987)

The two legged League Cup semi-final between the two went to a replay. Spurs had won the first leg away and were leading at half-time in the return fixture, when the Spurs PA announced how their fans could apply for Cup Final tickets. Incensed Arsenal players in their dressing room heard this and stormed back to force a replay, which they won, coming from behind, David Rocastle scoring in injury-time.

Tottenham 3 – 1 Arsenal (April, 1991)

The two teams met in the FA Cup semi-final that year with the Gunners chasing another double. But Paul Gascoigne and Gary Lineker inspired Spurs to a famous win.

Tottenham 2 – 2 Arsenal (April, 2004)

For the second time, Arsenal won the league at White Lane as their Invincibles side were en route to going through the entire 2003 – 2004 season unbeaten.

Crossing the divide

Eighteen players have appeared for both clubs and eight have played for both sides in the North London derby – *Laurie Brown, Sol Campbell, David Jenkins, Pat Jennings, Jimmy Robertson, Willie Young, William Gallas, and Emmanuel Adebayor.*

Current Tottenham star and England captain *Harry Kane* joined the Arsenal academy system aged just eight years old, but was released a year later.

There are managerial connections as well. The legendary *Herbert Chapman*, credited with making Arsenal the dominant team in English football in the 1930s, played for Spurs in his playing days.

George Graham, who was part of the Arsenal double winning team of the 1970 – 1971 season, went on to manage the club, steering them to two league titles, the FA Cup, the European Cup Winners Cup and two League Cups.

After he was fired by the Gunners over corruption allegations, he had three seasons in charge with Spurs, and won the League Cup with them.

Interesting facts about the rivalry

- The pair has yet to meet in a major final, although they have played three FA Cup and four League Cup semi-finals between them.
- Although Arsenal have won many more trophies than Spurs, when it comes to Europe, Spurs have the upper hand. They have won three European trophies to two for the Gunners. Both have been on the losing side in Champions League finals.
- Spurs were the first team in the modern era to win the League and Cup double in 1960 – 1961. A decade later Arsenal became the second, emulating the feat.
- Although it is sometimes claimed the Seven Sisters Road separates the two clubs, the road does not in fact go past the home ground of either.

THE OLD FIRM

CELTIC V RANGERS

Location: Glasgow, Scotland

First Meeting: 28 May 1888

Reported to be worth nearly US $200 million annually to the Scottish economy, the Old Firm derby between the two major Glasgow clubs, Celtic and Rangers, is one of the bitterest and hotly contested in the world. There are no half and half scarves sold for this game. No wonder all police leaves in Glasgow are cancelled in the days leading up to the derby day.

It is not just local pride or bragging rights that is at stake either. It is about politics, religion, differing social attitude and decades of history. It is impossible to separate this match from the politics and history of the UK and the neighbouring Ireland, and a victory for one side or the other usually has much deeper resonance beyond just the sporting arena.

The origins of the rivalry

The roots of the rivalry can be traced back as far as the 16th century, when Scotland, which had previously been a very pious Catholic nation, adopted Protestantism as a national religion.

Religious hostilities existed between the two communities for the next 300 years, exacerbated by a wave of (mainly Catholic) immigration from neighbouring Ireland in the 19th century, the immigrants bringing with them sectarian prejudices that soon infected local politics, workplaces and society in general.

Rangers were formed in 1872, and Celtic 15 years later. From the outset Celtic positioned themselves as the team of the immigrants, many of whom were not welcomed in mainly Protestant Scotland.

Despite this relations were initially cordial between the two clubs, with Rangers the first club Celtic ever played.

All that changed though, when the firm Harland and Wolff opened the enormous Govan shipyard in the early 1900s a short distance from Rangers' Ibrox ground. That brought a fresh wave of Protestant immigrants from Belfast to work in the docks, because the company had a strict "Catholics need not apply" employment rule.

This anti-Catholic prejudice spread to the local club the workforce adopted, and soon Rangers became associated with being conservative, and quickly became closely linked with Northern Ireland unionism (which favours close ties with Britain).

Meanwhile Celtic identified themselves with socialism and Irish Republicanism, one of whose avowed aims is to reunite the north of the country with the rest of Ireland, which is almost wholly Catholic.

Attitudes and beliefs soon became entrenched, handed down from generation to generation. Celtic supporters tend to celebrate their Irishness, whilst Rangers became staunchly anti-Catholic. The rivalry was given a fresh impetus when civil unrest broke out in Northern Ireland in the late 1960s, and the 30 years of troubles that followed only amplified the tensions on both sides of the divide.

For many years both clubs refused to sign players from the opposing faith. When Rangers ended their practice in 1989 by signing the forward Mo Johnston, he was given a hostile reception from fans of both clubs. Some Rangers fans burned scarves and threatened to throw away their season tickets, whilst Celtic supporters labelled him "Judas."

Meanwhile, Tommy Gemmell, one of the famous Lisbon Lions who had helped Celtic win the European Cup in 1967, and scored in the final against Inter Milan, still had to put up with sectarian abuse from a section of his own fans, because of his Protestant origins.

The rise of social media, opposing views about the thorny issue of Scottish independence, and the liquidation of the original Rangers' club in 2012, have only added more fuel to what is already a combustible mixture.

Notable Incidents

An encyclopaedia could be filled with notorious Old Firm incidents. The games between the two have seen numerous sending offs over the years, and are marked by acts of violence between fans, both on the day of the match, and in the days that follow and precede.

The 1980 Scottish Cup final resulted in a narrow win for Celtic but it was what happened afterwards that still lives in the memory. Dubbed as the "The Hampden Riot" when rival fans clashed and threw missiles at each other, and mounted police were deployed to restore order. Both clubs were fined heavily and a blanket ban on alcohol at all Scottish football grounds was imposed.

When Mo Johnston was signed by Rangers in 1989, all the club's players boycotted the press conference announcing his arrival. Jimmy Bell, the Rangers' kitman, refused to lay out Johnston's jersey before matches.

In 2002, Neil Lennon stopped playing international football for Northern Ireland after receiving death threats for being a catholic in a country dominated by Protestants. Less than a decade later, when he became manager of the Parkhead club, he was sent bullets and parcel bombs in the post.

A home win for Celtic in March 2011 saw Rangers finish with just eight men, and then, at the final whistle, Celtic manager Neil Lennon and Rangers assistant manager Ally McCoist tangled on the touchline and threw punches at each other.

Famous Games

Celtic 0 – 3 Rangers (May 1999)

This comprehensive away win for Rangers was overshadowed by a Celtic fan trying to attack referee Hugh Dallas, and when he was hustled away by stewards, a coin from the crowd struck Dallas, who fell to the floor. The image of him kneeling whilst he was attended by paramedics was beamed around the world.

A spectator was badly injured after falling from the top tier of one of the stands, and the Rangers players were attacked at the final whistle.

Rangers 2 – 2 Celtic (October 1987)

Football took a backseat in this match which saw three men not only sent off, but four of the names on the team sheet were subsequently charged with breach of the peace in the days that followed, after the Procurator Fiscal ordered a police enquiry into the game.

Celtic 2 - 0 Rangers (April 1998)

This match is best remembered not for the result or goals, but because Paul Gascoigne, who was playing for Rangers, mimed playing a flute, an instrument closely associated with Orange Order bands (an international Protestant fraternal order based in Northern Ireland).

Crossing the divide

At one time it was almost impossible for any player to consider appearing for both clubs. Five of those who did manage it – *David McLean, George Livingstone, Robert Campbell, Alex Bennett and Tully Craig* – did so before the Second World War, and it was many years before another player made the switch.

Alfie Conn was the next man to manage the feat, with an interlude with Spurs in between, followed by *Mo Johnston*. In recent years, it has become more common, and *Kenny Miller* became the first player to cross the divide twice.

Interesting facts about the rivalry

- The term "Old Firm" was coined from a famous headline which appeared in a Glasgow newspaper in the 1880s, referring to the clubs as "two, old firm friends". Any notion of friendship, though, disappeared long ago.
- The most successful manager in the history of Celtic was Jock Stein, who led them to the European Cup, ten league titles, eight Scottish Cups and six League Cups. But he was initially told he could not manage the club because he was a Protestant.
- The highest attendance for a league meeting between the two is 118,567 at Ibrox in January, 1939. It remains an all-time British record.
- A number of brothers have appeared for Celtic in derby matches against Rangers. The first pair were the Maley brothers who played in Celtic's first-ever match against Rangers back in 1888. Since then there have been the Dunbars (Tom and Michael), two pairs of McStays (Jimmy and Willie; Paul and Willie) and the O'Donnells (Frank and Hugh).

El Clasico

Real Madrid v Barcelona

Location: Spain

First Meeting: 13 May 1902

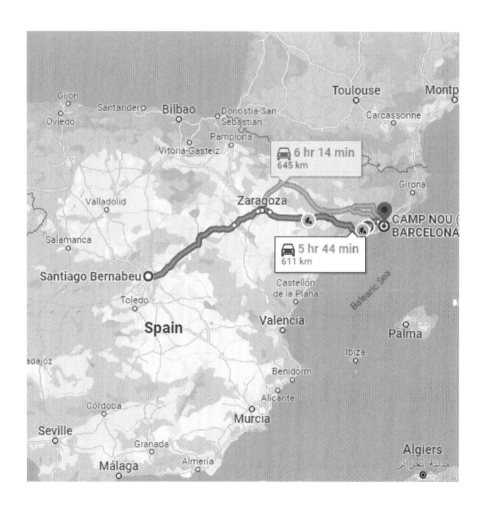

Due to its historical and cultural significance, the matches between Barcelona and Real Madrid are considered amongst the most intense and bitter ones in world football. El Clasico (the term used to describe games between the two) matches are the most watched domestic club football matches on the planet, with TV audiences running into the hundreds of millions.

The origins of the rivalry

The origins of the rivalry are inextricably linked with the events that have shaped the history of Spain since the turn of the 20th century. They owe to the fact, in part, that they are not just the two largest cities in the country, but also come from different provinces, Castile and Catalonia, each with their own language, culture, political affiliations and sense of identity.

The rivalry began to take shape as early as 1902, when one of their first meetings at a tournament in honour of King Alfonso XIII ended up with Barcelona winning, but Real Madrid blaming the loss on the six foreigners fielded by the opposition.

However, it was the Spanish civil war which raged between 1936 and 1939 which was to have a profound effect, and the ripples of which remain even to this day.

Backed by the major fascist powers of Europe, Adolf Hitler's Germany and Benito Mussolini's Italy, General Francisco Franco successfully led a coup against the Republican government which was based in Barcelona.

That led to a lasting resentment towards that region from Franco after he came to power, who was trying to demonstrate that a different culture or view of society under his rule would not be tolerated.

Real Madrid became known as Franco's club, and was associated with the status quo, and conservatism.

Meanwhile, with the growing popularity of football, FC Barcelona became an outlet for people to express their views and sentiments, especially those Catalans who were bitterly opposed to Franco and his policies. Barcelona became "mes que un club" (more than a club), not only for Catalans, but also for progressives and left-leaning Spaniards across the country.

Whilst Franco remained in power, there was a sense that the odds were always stacked in favour of Real, and, although he died in 1975, and a constitutional monarchy installed in his place, many of the fissures in Spanish society remain.

In 2017, the local parliament even passed a resolution that declared Catalonia independent from Spain and, although the uprising was subsequently quashed, underlying tensions remain.

Notable incidents

There have been numerous incidents over the years which have fuelled the rivalry.

In 1943, the two sides met in the semi-finals of the Copa del Generalisimo (a forerunner of the Copa del Rey). Barcelona won the first leg 3 – 0, but when they travelled to Madrid for the return fixture, the local press had provoked the Madrid fans so much so they were baying for Catalan blood.

Before the match, the Director of State Security visited the Barcelona dressing room and reminded the players about the government's generosity in allowing Catalonia to remain part of Spain.

Fearing for the safety of themselves and their families, Barcelona hardly put up a fight and Madrid hammered 11 goals past them, whilst goalkeeper Luis Miró spent most of the game terrified by the crowd behind his goal.

The Barcelona president at the time, Enrique Piñeyro Querall, was so disgusted that he resigned soon afterwards.

A major saga erupted in 1953 over the transfer of the Argentine footballer Alfredo di Stéfano, who had been playing in Colombia. Both clubs tried to sign him, but after a protracted dispute, FIFA ruled that Barcelona had won the race to his signature. Real then lobbied the government and as a consequence the Spanish football federation promptly banned the signing of any foreign players by Spanish clubs.

A compromise was then found permitting Di Stéfano to play two years for Real, and the following two years for Barcelona, However, on the orders of the Franco government, Barcelona backed out of the deal, enabling the Madrid club to become his sole employer.

Di Stéfano would go on to become the lynch pin of the side that won the first five European Cups.

Another transfer would put more petrol on the fire. Portuguese international Luis Figo was adored by the Barcelona fans during his time at the club, helping them win numerous trophies. The Catalans thought they had protected their investment by inserting a world record buy-out clause in his contract, only for Real Madrid to shock everybody by agreeing to meet it.

The previous darling was overnight transformed into a traitor. Figo was injured for the derby clash in Barcelona the season following his move, but the local fans had not forgotten the slight. And, when he did return, as he lined up to take a corner, he found a pig's head on the pitch next to him.

For more than a decade, El Clasico also provided a backdrop to another rivalry between Lionel Messi and Cristiano Ronaldo as to who was the best player in the world. By the time he left Barcelona for PSG, Messi had score 26 derby goals, eight more than his great rival.

Most famous matches

1961 European Cup First Round

Real Madrid had become the most dominant team in Europe in the 1950s, winning the European Cup in its first five years. Their defeat of Eintracht Frankfurt in the 1960 final is still regarded by some as the best ever performance by a club side.

It was fitting then that it was Barcelona who ended their long unending run in the competition the following year, drawing the away leg in Madrid, and winning 2 – 1 at home.

Barcelona 5 – 0 Real Madrid (January 1994)

Many argue that this was the crowning achievement for the Barcelona side that became known as the "Dream Team".

Real Madrid 5 – 0 Barcelona (January 1995)

Revenge was not only sweet but almost instant for Real fans the following year.

Champions League Semi-Final 2011

The rivalry reached almost unbearable heights when three derbies occurred in the space of just a few weeks towards the end of the 2010 – 2011 season. First there was a bad-tempered league game, and then a two legged Champions League semi-final. Jose Mourinho, the Real manager at the time, tried his best to get under the skin of his Barcelona counterpart, Pep Guardiola, but it was the Catalans who advanced to the final, where they beat Manchester United.

Crossing the divide

More than 30 players over the years have appeared for both clubs, without taking into account the case of Di Stéfano, who was denied the chance to put on both jerseys.

Apart from *Figo*, some notable examples are:

Ronaldo, the Brazilian striker, played one season for the Catalan club, but still managed to score 47 goals in just 49 appearances. He joined Real in 2002 as part of the Galácticos era, and won the league title with them.

Luis Enrique joined Real Madrid in 1991 and spent five seasons with them, but despite winning trophies in his time in the Spanish capital, he left on a free transfer claiming he was not appreciated. He promptly joined Barcelona where he soon became a fan favourite, and would later manage the club and the Spanish national side.

Michael Laudrup was signed by Johan Cruyff when he was the Barcelona manager, and he helped the Catalans win four consecutive league titles. A disagreement between the pair, however, promoted the Dane to switch allegiance, and he won the league title in his first season at the Bernabeu. Famously he played in two 5- 0 wins, one for each team.

Interesting facts about the rivalry

- The rivalry between the two is so intense that it has even developed its own vocabulary. For example, Canguelo is the expression used by the Madrid press to describe Barcelona's fear of losing the league to their rivals, whilst La Manita (little hand) refers to a 5 – 0 win by Barcelona. Meanwhile Madrid fans have been known to use the expression Villarato to describe how Barcelona seem to get favours from match officials.

- The term El Clasico was originally reserved for La Liga meetings between the two, but it has now been expanded to any encounter between the two great rivals.

- Despite the bitter rivalry between the two sets of fans, there have been instances when acts of sporting brilliance are mutually recognised. In 1983 during the Copa de Liga final, Barcelona star Diego Maradona was warmly applauded by Real fans when he allowed the opposing goalkeeper to get back into position after dribbling past him. And 22 years later in 2005, Ronaldinho was given a standing ovation at the Bernabeu after an outstanding game for the Catalan club.

DERBY DELLA MADONNINA

AC MILAN V INTER MILAN

Location: Milan, Italy

First Meeting: 10 January 1909

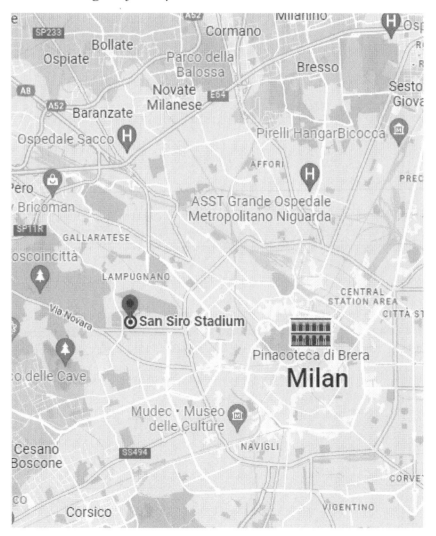

The Milan derby is one of the oldest in Italy, and one with a rich history and tradition. People in Milan either support AC or Inter, and whilst there may have originally been class or political differences between the two clubs, these have now been eroded by history.

The two share a stadium, the San Siro, although, strictly speaking it is the name of the district in which it is located, and it is really called the Giuseppe Meazza in honour of the World Cup winner who played for both clubs in the 20s, 30s, and 40s.

Although violence is not unknown at derby matches, they usually are devoid of the hooligan element that frequently mars Roma – Lazio clashes, for example. And that is because Milan and Inter fans will often work or go to school together.

The origins of the rivalry

AC Milan - the AC stands for Associazione Calcio (Football Association) were founded by a group of English expats, becoming one of the first football clubs in Italy.

Eight years into its existence, a bitter dispute among its members about the signing of foreign players, led to a split, and a group of them went away to form Internazionale (Inter for short).

The rivalry grew from that moment, although the reasons why somebody chooses to support either club varies.

There is a class element behind it. AC Milan fans were historically called casciavit (screwdrivers) because many of them were blue collar workers, and often economic migrants from southern Italy.

By contrast, Inter fans were called bauscia (boasters) because they were seen as white collar and entrepreneurs, and often came from the rich suburbs of Northern Milan.

For a time there was a political element to the rivalry as well, when AC Milan club president Silvio Berlusconi became a full-time politician and then Prime Minister. There is evidence, however, that some of those who did not share his centre-right leaning actually stopped supporting AC Milan for a while.

However, the main reason that somebody chose to support one or the other club is mainly family related. Allegiance is usually passed down from generation to generation, and people support the team that their fathers and grandfathers before them followed.

That is except for a small minority who will support the other team just to provoke other family members!

Notable incidents

In 2005 the two sides met in the quarter-final of the Champions League, Milan won the first leg 2 – 0, and then took the lead in the reverse fixture. Things then turned sour when Milan goalkeeper Dida was struck by a flare thrown from the stands and required treatment for first degree burns on his shoulder. Both sets of players pleaded with the fans to stop the chaos, but the German referee then decided to suspend the game. The players returned but with more flares raining down. The game was abandoned.

AC Milan were one of the clubs involved in the Calciopoli scandal in 2006, and were originally deducted 44 points that season, 15 points for the following season and kicked out of the Champion League, although this punishment was later reduced on appeal.

The prime beneficiaries of the scandal were Inter who, having seen their major rivals weakened, went on to dominate Italian football for the next few seasons. However, evidence has since come to light that Inter may have instigated the whole affair in the first place, when the first allegations appeared in the paper Gazetta dello Sport – popularly called Gazetta della Inter by rival fans.

The paper was owned at that time by Carlo Buora, who happened to be Inter's Vice President at the time.

During a derby loss to Inter in 2019 two Milan players started fighting each other on the bench. Franck Kessie, who had just been substituted, was visibly upset by the decision and had to be restrained after team mate Lucas Biglia said something to him.

Most famous matches

Inter 6 – 5 AC Milan (November 1949)

Not only was this the highest scoring match in the history of the derby, but it is remarkable for the fact that AC Milan were 4 – 1 up after just 19 minutes.

AC Milan 2 – 1 Inter (October 1984)

AC Milan's fortunes were at a low ebb in 1985. They had been demoted to Serie B in 1980 after a match fixing scandal, and then they suffered another relegation two years later. It had also been five years since they last won a derby, but a header from Englishman Mark Hateley brought that miserable run to an end.

Inter Milan 0 – 6 AC Milan (May 2001)

It is the biggest winning margin by either side in the history of the fixture, despite the fact that they had started the match level on points in table. Inter recovered from the humiliation to finish two points ahead of their rivals at the end of the season.

Inter 4 – 2 AC Milan (May 2012)

AC Milan had ended Inter's run of five successive titles in 2011, and seemed on course to defend the Scudetto when the two sides met in 2012. However, Diego Milito scored a hat-trick, and the defeat meant Juventus went on to win the title.

Crossing the divide

Despite the rivalry, there have been a number of players who have appeared for both clubs over the tears, including some of the most famous players of their era. Here are just a few from that list.

Mario Balotelli first made his name at Inter where he helped them win the treble in 2010 under Mourinho before moving on to Manchester City. When he returned to Italy in 2013 it was with AC Milan, and, for a time, he rediscovered his best form at the San Siro.

Zlatan Ibrahimović joined Inter when Juventus were relegated following the Calciopoli scandal. Inter won three successive Scudetto titles with him, before he was sold to Barcelona. But when he fell out with Pep Guardiola, he headed back to Milan, this time with AC Milan, winning a Serie A title with them.

He returned to the club for a second spell in 2020 winning yet another title with them.

Andrea Pirlo began his career with Brescia before moving to Inter, but he struggled to establish himself there. Joining AC Milan, however, he became one of their most famous players, winning two Serie A titles and two Champions League titles. He went on to have even more success with Juventus.

Inter signed Brazilian legend *Ronaldo* from Barcelona in 1997 for a then world record fee, and he would go to score 49 goals in 68 appearances for them, winning the Ballon d'Or, before signing for Real Madrid for another record sum. He returned to Milan with AC after five years in Spain. Although past his best he still showed touches of brilliance before injuries forced him to retire in his second season.

Interesting facts about the rivalry

- The first match between the pair in 1908 did not even take place in Italy. It was played in Chiasso, Switzerland, AC Milan winning 2 – 1.
- The name Derby della Madonnina was chosen in honour of the statue of the Virgin Mary that adorns the top of Milan Cathedral.
- AC Milan are known as Rossoneri (red and blacks) and Inter Milan Nerazzuri (Blue and Blacks).
- Inter Milan won their first Scudetto in 1910, but the captain of their team, who was also their coach, Virgilio Fossati, was killed in action in the First World War.

SUPERCLÁSICO

BOCA JUNIORS V RIVER PLATE

Location: Buenos Aires, Argentina

First Meeting: 24 August 1913

Arguably no rivalry in world football is more intense than that between the Buenos Aires pair of Boca Juniors and River Plate. Despite more than 100 years of history between them, there is no sign of the relationship mellowing with age, as the authorities struggle to maintain order between the warring sides.

When the pair met in the final of the two-legged Copa Libertadores in 2018, so bad was the violence after the first match that the second leg had to be relocated to Madrid, some 10,000 kilometres away to try and prevent a repeat.

And with more than 70% of all Argentinian football fans claiming allegiance to one club or the other, matches between the two truly divide the nation.

Meanwhile, for football supporters abroad, attending a Superclásico once in their lifetime remains high on the bucket list, only to experience the feeling of being in a stadium that literally shakes as thousands of people bounce up and down.

The origins of the rivalry

River Plate were founded in 1901, with Boca coming into being four years later. Both teams originated from the same neighbourhood in Buenos Aires, La Boca, a working class area near the Riachuelo's mouth. It has a strong Italian culture, with many of its early settlers from the city of Genoa.

From the outset there was a strong local rivalry, with the first derby taking place in 1913, which was won by River Plate.

In 1925, however, River Plate made the decision to relocate to the wealthier neighbourhood of Núñez, a move that led to them acquiring the nickname "Los Millonarios (the Millionaires) after which they began to sign the best players in the country following the advent of professionalism in 1931.

Boca stayed put, and quickly became known as the team of the working class, with many of their supporters coming from the immigrant communities.

Notable incidents

In 1968, the two teams met in the 89th derby, when a major stadium tragedy occurred at River Plate's Monumental Stadium. People trying to exit the ground found gate 12 locked, but people at the top of the stairs did not realise what had happened and continued to push their way down. Somebody tripped, precipitating a mass crush. 71 people died and more than 150 injured in the worst sporting disaster in the history of Argentina. An official inquiry failed to pin the blame on any one party.

In 2012 River Plate fans floated a giant inflatable pig wearing a Boca shirt above the away section of their home ground.

In 2015, during a Copa Libertadores match, Boca fans attacked the River Plate players using pepper spray. A number of the players were injured in the incident, and their team was subsequently awarded the tie.

Arguably the flash point though was the 2018 Libertadores final. After the two teams had played out a two-all draw in La Bombonera, Boca's ground, the second leg was due to take place a few days later. However, River fans threw objects at the Boca bus carrying the players, and tear gas was fired by police in a bid to restore order.

When the Boca players finally reached their destination, they claimed they were not in a fit state to play the game. The start of the game was delayed twice and then eventually cancelled, and then rescheduled to the next day. That too was cancelled, and the decision eventually made to stage it in Madrid instead.

Most famous matches

Boca Juniors 3 – 0 River Plate (April 1981)

Maradona could have been a River Plate player when he left Argentinos Juniors, but he chose Boca instead, and he showed the full extent of his burgeoning talent in this derby victory which he marked with an iconic goal.

Boca Juniors 0 – 2 River Plate (April 1986)

River had already secured the league title when this match took place. Their players, despite a request from the Argentine president at the time, still chose to celebrate with a lap of hour prior to kick off at La Bombonera, infuriating the Boca fans.

The match became known as the 'Orange Ball Superclásico' because so many white papers were thrown on to the pitch that they had to use an orange ball so it could be seen.

River Plate 2 - 1 Boca Juniors (June 2004)

The two met in the semi-finals of the Copa Libertadores, and Boca won the first leg by a single goal. They went behind in the second leg but thought they had won the tie when Carlos Tevez scored for them. He was sent off for his celebration which saw him imitate a chicken, and River Plate scored again to force extra time and penalties. 10 men Boca won the shoot-out.

Crossing the divide

Given the intense rivalry between the two sides, it is surprising that anybody has made the journey between the two clubs, let alone the nearly 100 "traitors" that have actually done it.

Among the most famous are:

Gabriel Batistuta nicknamed 'Batigol" played one season for River Plate and then joined their rivals, scoring 19 goals before moving to Europe where he became a superstar.

Another Argentine international striker, *Claudio Caniggia* began his career with River Plate, before moving to Italy and then Benfica in Portugal. He returned to Argentina with Boca for three seasons and his later career included spells in Scotland with Dundee and Rangers.

Jorge Higuain, the father of Gonzalo Higuain was a defender who played a season with Boca, and then spent three years with River Plate for whom he made 131 appearances.

Interesting facts about the rivalry

- Few expected the rivalry to end, but it did, briefly on the football field, when River Plate were relegated at the end of the 2010 – 2011 season (it is known by River fans as "the wound that will never heal."). Predictably this delighted Boca supporters who began to call the red and white side "Riber", the popular name for the Argentine second division.

- Both sets of fans taunt their rivals with insults. Boca call River "Gallinas" (chickens) because they say their players lack guts. However, River Plate fans respond with terms like "Bosteros" (manure collectors) and "Los chanchitos" (little pigs) because they claim that the La Boca area of the city smells bad.

- Fans of both sides report that they do not like derby day because of the stress that it causes. There have been a number of heart attacks reported and even deaths.

INTERCONTINENTAL

FENERBAHCE V GALATASARAY

Location: Istanbul, Turkey

First Meeting: 17 January 1909

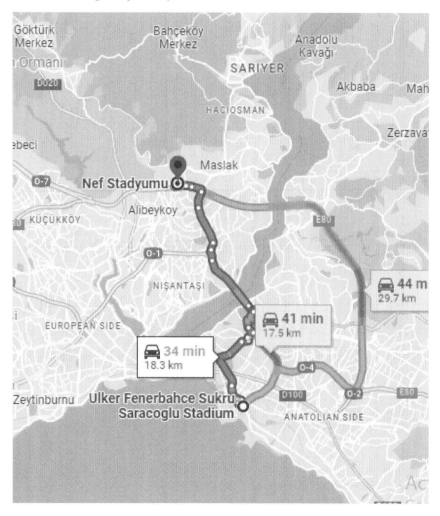

Istanbul in Turkey is unique because it straddles two continents, separated as it is by the Bosporus strait, a waterway that connects the Sea of Marmara and the Black Sea. West of the strait, and in Europe, is the city's commercial and historic centre, and the areas most visited by tourists. To the east, and in Asia, are mainly residential districts.

About two thirds of the city's population is in Europe, and one third in Asia, although the numbers are continually fluctuating as the city expands.

The Bosporus also provides a barrier between two of Turkey's most illustrious football clubs, with Galatasaray in Europe, and Fenerbahçe in Asia.

The origins of the rivalry

Galatasaray were founded in 1905 by a group of students from Galatasaray High School, one of the city's most prestigious learning institutions.

Two years later Fenerbahçe were created with money supplied from the west, and was regarded as a symbol of an economically thriving and rapidly growing Asian Turkey.

Its links with Asia were further strengthened by its affiliation with Mustafa Kemal Ataturk, who is regarded as the father of modern Turkey because of his role in fighting for independence after the collapse of the Ottoman Empire.

Ataturk was a well-known Fener fan.

Many pinpoint the exact start of the rivalry to February 1934 when, what was meant to be a friendly between the two clubs quickly deteriorated as hard tackles rained in on both sides, leading to a mass brawl on the pitch. The referee was left with no choice but to abandon the game.

The rivalry today has taken on other dimensions, between western secular Turkey, and the Asian part of the country which is more Islamist in its leanings. Nor is it confined just to Istanbul. Violent incidents between fans have become common in recent years, and cover the gamut from breaking seats, fightings, stabbings, fireworks and even riots. It is not uncommon for fights between rival groups to break out across Turkey just before, or on, derby day itself.

Notable incidents

In the 1995 – 1996 season the two teams reached the final of the Turkish cup. Fenerbahçe were the much stronger team at the time, but instead it was Galatasaray who won the first leg of the final. Their manager at the time, Graeme Souness, planted a huge Galatasaray flag in the centre of the pitch. It sparked a riot and incensed Fener fans rained objects down on the pitch and at the fleeing Souness.

In 2006 Galatasaray fans unfurled a huge racist banner which targeted Mehmet Aurélio, a popular player with Fenerbahçe and the Turkish national team, who had Brazilian roots. When Fenerbahçe fans protested they were attacked by large groups of Galatasaray ultras.

In May 2013 a 16-year old Fenerbahçe fan was on his way home after a derby match, when he and the friends he was walking with, came under attack by a group of opposing fans. He was stabbed multiple times and died at the scene.

In February 2020, Fenerbahçe's unbeaten home run in the fixture, which had lasted 21 years, finally came to an end. When Galatasaray scored their third in the seventh minute of added time, Fener president Ali Koc began arguing with his own fans, and even jumped to the tier below his seat so he could carry on fighting.

The following year a Fenerbahçe fan tried to assault Galatasaray executive Abdurrahim Albayrak, only to be beaten up by his body guards.

Most famous matches

Fenerbahçe 0 – 7 Galatasaray (February 1911)

Galatasaray started this match with only six players, because heavy storm meant the rest of the squad could no cross the Bosphorus by ferry. A seventh joined them after the match started, but Fener finished with only six players themselves due to injury.

Fenerbahçe 4 - 4 Galatasaray (February 2001)

The highest scoring game in the history of the fixture, the hosts took a 3 – 1 lead and then led 4 – 2 only for the visitors to come storming back. Fenerbahce won 7 – 6 on penalties.

Fenerbahce 6 – 0 Galatasaray (November 2002)

Fenerbahce's biggest ever winning margin in this fixture is actually more remarkable because that season they finished 26 points behind their hated rivals in the Super Lig.

Fenerbahce 0 – 0 Galatasaray (May 2012)

This was the only time a play-off system was used to determine the destiny of the league title. Galatasaray needed just a draw to pip their rivals. They managed it after a match featuring two red cards, and fighting throughout the game off the pitch and on it.

With Galatasaray winning the title in the end, home fans ran onto the pitch. Riot police were called in and Fenerbahçe executives turned off the lights in the stadium to bring an end to the scenes of jubilation.

Crossing the divide

Compared to many rivalries there has been quite a lot of traffic between the two clubs over the years, and they have six managers in common, including Englishman *Peter Molloy* who had two years at Galatasaray between 1947 and 1949, before heading eastwards.

The most recent player to switch allegiance is Portuguese winger Bruma. He joined Galatasaray from Sporting Lisbon in 2013, and made 57 appearances for them, before spells with RB Leipzig and PSV, he joined Fenerbahce on loan in 2022.

Interesting facts about the rivalry

- In 1912 it was agreed by the presidents of both clubs that they would merge to create an Istanbul "super-club" called Turkkulubu. They had gone as far as agreeing the kit design for the new club, but the Balkan Wars then broke out before the proposal could be carried out.
- A 2011 poll asked 1.4 million Turks who they supported. 35% of them identified themselves as Galatasaray fans, 34% opting for Fenerbahçe.
- In terms of global support, Fenerbahçe are more popular in Muslim countries, whilst Galatasaray have a bigger European following.

THE NORTHWEST DERBY

LIVERPOOL V MANCHSTER UNITED

Location: North West England

First Meeting: 28 April 1894

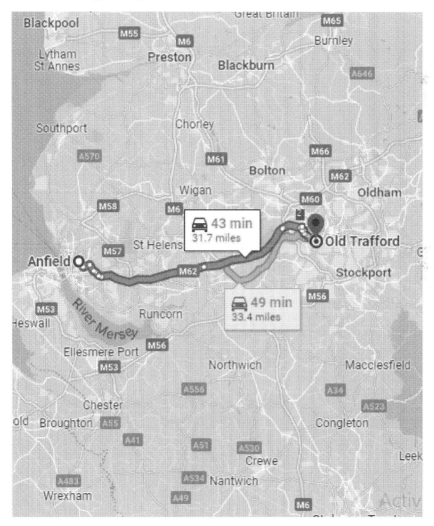

The Liverpool and Manchester United rivalry is one of the biggest, not only in English but world football, and has also become one of the most toxic. Both clubs have local rivalries with city neighbours – Everton in the case of Liverpool and City in the case of Manchester United – but the enmity when the two clubs face each other is of a new level.

And it transcends just the North-West of England. One of the reasons cited for England's so-called generation failing to reach their full potential was that, when Liverpool and United players found themselves on international duty together, they would barely talk to each other.

The origin of this mutual antipathy though goes back many years.

The origins of the rivalry

The rivalry between the two clubs reflects a deeper and long lasting enmity between the cities of Liverpool and Manchester which can be traced back to the Industrial Revolution.

By the late 18th century, Liverpool had established itself as a major seaport, whilst Manchester thrived due to its many textile factories. However, in order to get goods out to valuable export markets overseas, they had to route them all via Liverpool, who charged them heavy duties.

In a bid to avoid these additional costs, in 1894 Manchester constructed a ship canal, a 36 mile long inland waterway which connected the city directly to the Irish Sea. It gave ocean going vessels direct access to Manchester and enabled them to miss out Liverpool altogether.

Predictably the bill to approve the necessary legislation to approve the building of the canal faced heavy opposition from Liverpool supporters in parliament, but it was eventually passed. As they had feared, its construction turned out to have devastating economic consequences for Liverpool, and many jobs were lost in the port, and in industries that relied on it.

Despite that the cities have much in common, with both having long traditions of opposing the London ruling elite through political and trade union agitation.

And, in more recent times, buses full of Scousers, as people from Liverpool are called, would head to Manchester on a Saturday night in the 1950s and

1960s, lured by its pubs, live music and cinema halls, whilst Mancunians would take the reverse journey to Liverpool attracted by its thriving music scene.

These cross-city trips would often end up in bloody punch-ups.

Football, though took the rivalry to new levels. Between them they dominated the league landscape, Liverpool in the 1970s and 1980s, and United under Sir Matt Busby and Sir Alex Ferguson. And, since then, the mutual dislike between the supporters of both clubs has been elevated to a new level.

Notable incidents

A 2006 FA Cup match between the two clubs at Anfield saw various objects thrown at United fans by the home support, including human excrement.

In February 2012, Liverpool striker Luis Suárez refused to shake the hand of United full-back Patrice Evra pre-match because he had been banned for eight matches for racially abusing Evra the last time the two sides had met. Evra celebrated right in front of the Uruguayan after United won the match, but he was pushed and shoved by Liverpool players.

In March 2016, the two clubs met in the League Cup semi-final played over two legs. Before the first leg at Anfield a banner saying 'Manc Bastards' was hung on the M62 motorway, which links the two cities. For the reverse fixture, Liverpool supporters were greeted with a similar banner saying "Murderers". During the game, seats were ripped up and supporters fought and threw seats at each other.

It is impossible to discuss the rivalry without referencing the unpleasant singing indulged in by certain sections of the respective fanbases. Liverpool fans like to taunt their rivals by reminding them of the Munich air crash in 1958, in which 8 of the "Busby Babes" died, along with staff members and accompanying journalists. Equally unpleasantly, United fans will reference the Hillsborough disaster of 1989 when 96 Liverpool fans were crushed to death.

Most famous matches

Liverpool 1 – 2 Manchester United (May 1977)

This was the first time they had met in the final of a major trophy (*FA Cup*). Liverpool had just won the league but United denied them the chance to complete the double by winning 2 – 1

Liverpool 2 – 1 Manchester United (March 1983)

Liverpool got their revenge six years later, winning 2 – 1 in the League Cup final in what proved to be the final season in charge for Bob Paisley, who had led them to unprecedented success.

Manchester United 1 – 0 Liverpool (May 1996)

The pair met again in the FA Cup final in 1996, only to be decided by Eric Cantona's late winner for United. The Liverpool players were dubbed the "Spice Boys" for the white suits they wore before the match.

Manchester United 0 – 5 (October 2021)

Liverpool inflicted on United their heaviest ever home defeat in the fixture, thrashing them 5 – 0 at Old Trafford. Ole Gunnar Solskjaer would lose his job as manager shortly afterwards.

Crossing the divide

Given the rivalry between the two clubs, there have only been a handful of players who have appeared in the colours of both teams.

Tom Chorlton

Defender Chorlton's move from Liverpool to United was the first direct transfer between the two clubs back in 1912. He had spent nearly eight years at Anfield before switching allegiance on the eve of the First World War.

Phil Chisnall

Chisnall's claim to fame is that he is the last direct transfer between the two teams, and that was back in 1964. The forward had scored eight goals in 35 appearances for United, before signing for Bill Shankly's team.

However, facing intense competition at Anfield, he played just six games for the Kop before he was sold to Southend United.

Paul Ince

"The Governor" as he was known, Ince began his career with West Ham before joining United in 1989. He would go on to make 281 appearances for them, scoring 28 times, and winning six major trophies, including a league and cup double, before heading to Italy with Inter Milan.

When that did not work out as planned he returned to England and signed for Liverpool, where he remained for two seasons. He is the only man to have captained both clubs.

Peter Beardsley

Although Beardsley is best remembered for his time with Newcastle and Liverpool, for whom he scored 61 goals, he did make one appearance in a United shirt.

Michael Owen

Owen burst on to the scene as a teenager at Liverpool, and played a vital part in Liverpool's cup treble winning season in 2001, the same year he won the Ballon d'Or. A spell at Real Madrid followed, although he was already suffering from the injuries that would stay with him for the rest of his career.

He returned to England with Newcastle, but then signed for United as a free agent in 2009, earning the undying enmity of some Liverpool fans. He won a Premier League medal with United and, although he only scored 17 goals for them, one was the winner in a Manchester derby which endeared him to the Old Trafford faithful.

Interesting facts about the rivalry

- Back in 1915, a game between the two was at the centre of match fixing allegations. Four players from Liverpool and three from United were banned for life, after being found guilty of helping to contrive a result that saw United avoid relegation.
- Manchester United beat Liverpool 5-0 in a First Division clash back in 1946, and did so at Maine Road, Manchester City's home

ground. Old Trafford was destroyed during the Second World War, meaning United had to share ground with City.

- United's legendary manager Sir Matt Busby was a Liverpool player and could've also the Merseyside giants, having been offered a job as assistant manager, but he went to Manchester United instead, as they allowed him more control over the team.

DE KLASSIEKER

AJAX V FEYENOORD

Location: Netherlands

First Meeting: 9 October 1921

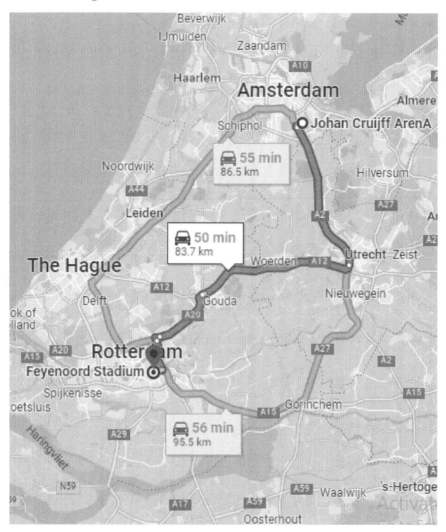

De Klassieker remains the most fiercely contested derby in the Netherlands, between the two clubs that are regarded as the biggest, despite the rise to prominence of PSV Eindhoven in the 1970s and 1980s, and, to a lesser extent, Alkmaar and Arnhem.

It is the one Dutch domestic fixture that attracts interest from rest of Europe, and, like many derbies it has its roots in differences - historical, cultural, economic, social, and philosophical - between the two cities of Amsterdam and Rotterdam.

The origins

The two emerged as the best teams in the country in the early years of Dutch football and, although Ajax have enjoyed considerably more success in recent years than Feyenoord, the rivalry between the two clubs and sets of supporters remains undiminished.

As is often the case, the animosity between the two clubs is actually a projection into the sporting arena of a deeper and longer standing rivalry between two cities, Rotterdam and Amsterdam, which although just 36 miles apart in distance, sometimes seem much further than that culturally.

Feyenoord is in the industrial heartland of the country, and has one of the biggest ports in Europe. It, therefore, regards itself as the club of the working man.

Amsterdam, by contrast, is viewed as a cultural city for tourists, and people who live there are regarded as lazy and arrogant by the people of Rotterdam, and viewed with suspicion by the rest of the country holding liberal views and tendencies at odds with their innate conservatism.

As one Rotterdammer wrote "Holland's money is earned in Rotterdam, divided in The Hague, and flushed down the toilet in Amsterdam."

And, like many western industrial cities, Rotterdam has seen its fair share of job losses since the 1960s, whilst Amsterdam is more associated with "white collar" employment.

There is also an unfortunate religious connotation to the rivalry as well. Ajax are widely regarded as a Jewish club because they have a large number of supporters from that faith. It is not uncommon to see Star of David flags waved at their matches, whilst favourite players can be encouraged with slogans like "joden" or "yid."

That has led to widespread antisemitic chanting directed at them by Feyenoord fans, often with particular emphasis to the Second World War, when three-quarters of the country's Jewish population were deported and killed in Nazi death camps. And there have also been cries of "Hamas, Hamas" at some games.

Ajax fans are no angels either, and any reference to Feyenoord players on social media often includes hashtags referring to #BombenopRotterdam (Bombs on Rotterdam). This is clear reference to the heavy bombing the city suffered during the Second World War (Amsterdam was barely affected).

There is also undeniably a sense of envy – Ajax have become the most famous club in the Netherlands and Feyenoord are becoming increasingly sick of living in their shadows.

Notable Incidents

Because of the rivalry between the two cities and clubs, there has been a history of bad blood between the two sets of fans. In 2004, during a reserve game between the two teams, a Feyenoord player Jorge Acuna had to be admitted to a hospital after he was ambushed by an Ajax "firm".

However, the most infamous incident between the two sets of fans had occurred seven years earlier in the small town of Beverwijk near Amsterdam. That was when rival gangs clashed violently, leaving one Ajax fan dead, whilst many more were injured.

Since then, local police have taken measures to keep the rival fan groups apart on match days. Now police ensure that travelling fans are escorted from buses and trains to stadiums on match days when the two teams meet.

To also try and limit the possibilities of violence, in February 2009, the mayors of Amsterdam and Rotterdam made an agreement with the KNVB (Dutch Football Association) to ban fans from away games.

As a consequence the occurrence of violent outbreaks has decreased, even if it will never go away completely.

However, as recently as 2016, the Ajax ultra -group VAK 410 were banned from the home game against Feyenoord because they had hung an effigy of former Ajax goalkeeper Kenneth Vermeer, playing for their hated rivals, from the main stand.

Three years later, an amateur game between AVV Swift from Amsterdam and SC Feyenoord was gate crashed by hooligans of both sides, and eventually it had to be played behind closed doors.

Most famous matches

Ajax 8 – 2 Feyenoord (September 1983)

This was the biggest defeat ever suffered by Feyenoord in this fixture, and was a match marred by crowd violence, both inside the ground and in the surrounding area.

Feyenoord 4 – 1 Ajax (February 1984)

The reverse fixture that season saw Feyenoord get their revenge en route to the league and cup double. Johan Cruyff got one of the goals for Feyenoord, to his delight as he sought personal vengeance for being released by the Amsterdam club at the end of the previous season.

Crossing the divide

There are a number of players who have turned up for both clubs, whilst four men have had spells managing the two teams. Famous names include the likes of *Johnny Rep, Ronald Koeman, and Leo Beenhakker.*

Johan Cruyff though, is arguably the best example. Indelibly linked with the great Ajax team of the late 1960s and early 70s that epitomised the concept of total football under coach Rinus Michels and won three consecutive European Cups, Cruyff had left the Netherlands for Barcelona, where he was to have an equally revolutionary impact.

However, after three years in the USA and a brief spell with Levante, he returned to Ajax and helped them achieve even more success. When, though, they declined to offer him a new contract, at the end of the 1982 – 1983, he was both offended and infuriated.

Determined to prove them wrong, he decided to sign for arch rivals Feyenoord instead, choosing not to accept a salary but instead insisting on a share of the gate receipts.

Cruyff had the last laugh. In his one season in Rotterdam, he helped Feyenoord to a league and cup double.

Interesting facts about the rivalry

- Although the first match between the two clubs in Rotterdam in October 1921 ended in an Ajax win, the result was later declared a draw after Feyenoord protested against the award of a dubious goal to the visitors.
- Between 1948 and 1956 no competitive matches were played between the two clubs because Feyenoord were unable to win their regional league during this period.
- Although Ajax are by far the most successful Dutch team in the history of European football, it was actually Feyenoord who were the first side from that country to win the European Cup, when they beat Celtic in the final in 1970.
- The rivalry even extended as far as who had the bigger stadium. When Feyenoord's De Kuip stadium was completed in 1937, Ajax added another tier to theirs the same year. Feyenoord responded by expanding De Kuip after the war.

Derby D'Italia

Juventus v Inter Milan

Location: Northwest Italy

First Meeting: 14 November 1909

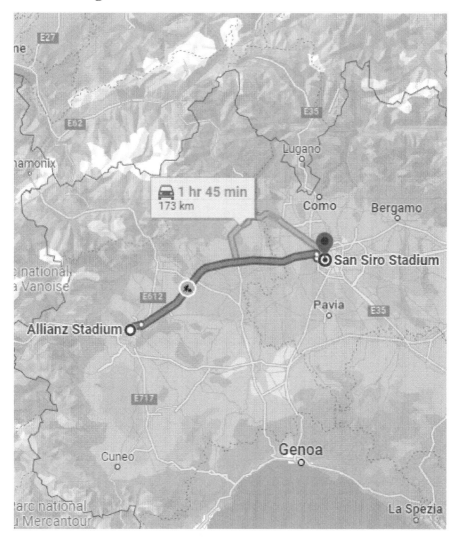

In a country famed for its rivalries, Derby d'Italia is the most intense rivalry in Italy between teams from different cities, Turin and Milan, which are located 91 miles from each other.

It is a fierce rivalry that is rooted in the history of the two clubs, who, along with AC Milan, are the most successful in the history of Italian football. However, what was already deep animosity between the two clubs and sets of supporters was given even more impetus after a scandal that rocked Italian football to its core.

The origins of the rivalry

Although the origin of the rivalry is a matter of debate, many point to the events of the 1960/61 season as a major catalyst. In April of that year, second placed Inter travelled to Turin for a match against the league leaders knowing that a win would enable them to close the gap at the top.

However, due to extreme overcrowding, with thousands of fans spilling out of the stands to watch the match from the side-lines, the game was called off by the referee after just half an hour on safety grounds.

According to the prevailing rules at the time, Inter were awarded a 2 – 0 win, but Juventus objected to this and appealed to the Italian Football Federation (whose head at the time was, coincidentally, also the President of Juventus). They eventually ruled that the result would not stand and ordered the game to be replayed.

Inter reluctantly agreed, but, as a form of protest, fielded their B team instead, who were thrashed 9 – 1.

It was the Calciopoli scandal that really took things to a new level, though. It happened during the 2004 – 2005 following an extensive investigation which included the hidden recording of bugged telephone conversations by law enforcement officers. They revealed Juventus general manager Luciano Moggi and other club representatives having conversations with officials from the Italian football federation to influence the appointment of referees, and to ensure only those predisposed to the Turin club would referee Juventus matches.

AC Milan, Fiorentina, Lazio and Reggina were all implicated in the scandal, but it was Juventus who were seen as the main culprits and suffered the heaviest punishment. They were stripped of the league title they won in the

2004 – 2005 season, and relegated to Serie B. Meanwhile, they were downgraded to last place in the 2005 – 2006 season and the title was awarded to second place Inter Milan instead.

Juventus have never accepted the decision. They have appealed more than 30 times to have their title restored to them, but all their claims have been objected.

Even today they wear 3 stars on their shirts to signify the 30 Serie A titles they have won – 1 star for every 10 championships – even though the record books say they have only won 29.

As a codicil there is evidence to suggest that Calciopoli was, in part, engineered by Inter's president at the time, Massimo Moratti, with the news of the scandal first published by Gazetta dello Sport (popularly known as Gazetta dello Inter by rival fans).

Notable Incidents

Referee Piero Ceccarini has become synonymous with the Derby d'Italia, with the footage of the penalty he refused to award Inter in the match in the 1997 – 1998 season almost as famous as the shooting of JFK.

Even today, many Inter fans swear blindly they were robbed after Ronaldo was body checked by defender Mark Iuliano as he bore down on goal.

To make matters worse, the referee waved play on and at the other end, a clumsy challenge saw Juventus awarded a spot kick instead. It was missed, but with Juventus already leading, held on for the win and they went on to secure the league title.

Emotions continued to run high and a fight broke out in the Italian parliament a week later, with right-wing politician Domenico Gramazio clashing with former Juventus player Massimo Mauro.

Conspiracy theorists note that Inter were the only top club not to be indicted at the time of Calciopoli scandal, with suggestions that the evidence in the case may have been fabricated by Telecom Italia, a company with personal and commercial interest in Inter.

Most famous matches

Inter 6 – 0 Juventus (April 1954)

This was a top of the table clash at the climax of the 1953/1954 season. Victory for Inter not only helped them win the Scudetto that year, but it remains their biggest margin of victory over their rivals.

Inter 1 – 1 Juventus (October 2002)

For 90 minutes almost nothing of note happened, and then it all kicked off. A foul on Alessandro del Piero in the final moments gave Juventus a penalty. Two players saw red for some fisticuffs, and Juventus scored from the spot. Five minutes into injury time, Inter won a corner, which goalkeeper Francesco Toldo contested, getting the vital touch that led to the equaliser.

Juventus 3 – 0 Inter (March 2003)

The two sides were locked together on 48 points at the top of the Serie A table at the start of the match, but, by the time it was over, Juventus were well on their way to another league title.

Inter 1 – 2 Juventus (March 2008)

This victory was particularly sweet for Juventus as it was the first meeting between the two sides after the Calciopoli scandal.

Crossing the divide

There have actually been a number of players who have appeared for both teams over the years. Here are just a few.

Guiseppe Meazza

Inter's San Siro Stadium is actually named after Meazza, who scored 282 goals for them between 1927 and 1940. He crossed the city to play for Milan, and then joined Juventus two years later.

Patrick Vieira

Although best remembered for his time at Arsenal, the French midfielder joined the club from AC Milan, and then left for Juventus in 2005. When they were relegated to Serie B after the Calciopoli scandal, he switched to Inter and won four consecutive league titles there.

Roberto Baggio

The man voted Italy's Player of the 20th century, Baggio was at the peak of his career when he played for Juventus between 1990 and 1995. He then moved to Inter and remained there for two seasons.

Zlatan Ibrahimović

Ibrahimović made his first foray into Italian football when he joined Juventus from Ajax in 2004. Part of the side that had two league titles stripped after Calciopoli, like Vieira he left rather than be relegated to Serie B, joining Inter, where he won three Serie A titles.

Interesting facts about the rivalry

- Both clubs were initial members of the European Super League that was announced in April 2021. Inter, after a heavy backlash from their own supporters withdrew within 48 hours, along the six Premier League clubs and Atlético Madrid. Juventus are still pursuing the ESL.
- No team has a better record in terms of wins against a single opponent in the history of Serie A than Juventus have against Inter.
- Although Juventus are the most successful club in the history of Italian football, Inter have won more European trophies than their rivals.

THE EDINBURGH DERBY

HEARTS V HIBS

Location: Edinburgh, Scotland

First Meeting: 25 December 1875

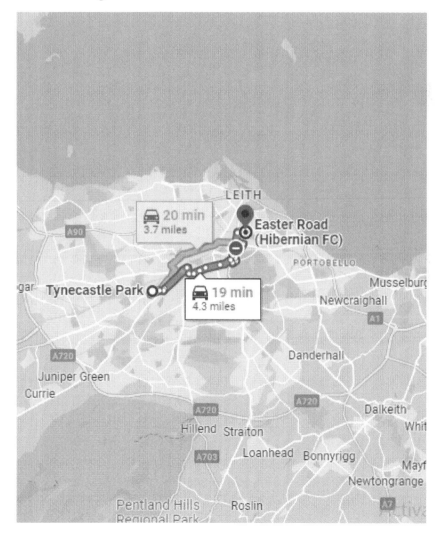

Whilst Edinburgh may be best known globally for its international arts festival and its Hogmanay celebrations which attract millions of tourists every year, for the local population football is an abiding passion, and most would identify themselves as either a Jam Tart or Hibbie with little in between.

Just like in Glasgow, the rivalry of Edinburgh's two biggest clubs - Heart of Midlothian and Hibernian – is mired in religious and sectarian divisions, although matches lack some of the extreme violence that have marred clashes between the West Scotland rivals.

It has been some time since either club has been challenging for major honours in Scotland, but that has done nothing to lessen the intensity when the two teams meet.

The origins of the rivalry

Both clubs were formed in the 1870s, beginning with Hearts who got their name because the original founders were all members of the Heart of Midlothian Quadrille Assembly, a dancing club. Hibernian were formed a year later by Irish immigrants.

The two grounds are three miles apart.

Although, not to the same extent as the animus between Celtic and Rangers, but there was undoubtedly a sectarian element to the rivalry between the two clubs. Hearts were always regarded as the Protestant club, whilst the fact that Hibs were established by Irish immigrants meant that they became associated with Catholics. This is reflected in the green of the club's badge, and the fact that they wear similar colours to Celtic.

For a time in the early part of the 1890s the rivalry was suspended because financial problems forced Hibs to stop playing matches altogether. But, when they were able to resume playing again, their first match was against Hearts.

Notable Incidents

The game between the pair on New Year's Day in 1940 featured 11 goals and numerous near-misses and great saves. The problem was that few of the 14,000 people inside Tynecastle Park could actually see anything because the ground was shrouded in thick fog.

It also left radio commentator Bob Kingsley with a dilemma, because he could only actually see two players when the match kicked off. Kingsley tried to solve his problems by employing a series of runners to bring him back information on what was going on from the touchline, but things soon became muddled. Instead, Kingsley ad-libbed and described an entirely make believe match full of incident.

In the early 1990s, Wallace Mercer, the owner of Hearts, tried to force through a merger of the two clubs after becoming a majority shareholder in Hibs. This led to a heightening of tensions among supporters, and culminated in a match at Easter Road that saw violent clashes between the fans.

There had already been a pitch invasion, when, with Hearts winning, the police entered both dressing rooms at half-time and asked if neither side could score in the second-half to ensure things did not get out of hand completely.

Mercer was forced to abandon his plans because of fan protests.

Thirteen years later, referee Stuart Dougal was on the end of an attack by a disgruntled supporter, unhappy with his decisions during a derby match. His assailant was a 38-year old care worker who leapt on to the pitch from an area of the ground reserved for disabled supporters. The fan was later banned for life.

Most famous matches

Hearts 8 – 3 Hibs (September 1935)

This match remains the heaviest competitive defeat that Hearts have inflicted on their neighbours.

Hearts 0 – 7 Hibs (January 1973)

Hibs began the New Year of 1973 in the best possible way by inflicting this record defeat on their rivals from across the city. Had it not been a Man of the Match performance by goalkeeper Kenny Garland, then the score line might have been even worse for Hearts.

Hibs 0 – 4 Hearts (May 2006)

This was a Scottish Cup semi-final played at Hampden Park, with Hearts running out easy winners against a Hibs side that finished with only nine men. Hearts would go on to beat non-league Gretna in the final.

Hearts 5 – 1 Hibs (May 2012)

In 2012 the pair met in Scottish Cup Final, again at Hampden Park. It proved to be a bad day at the office for Hibs, who were out-played for much of the match.

Crossing the divide

In total, there have been 39 players who have played for both clubs so far, with switching allegiance not carrying the same taboo as the Glasgow rivalry.

Gordon Smith made his debut for Hibs against Hearts, and became an instant hero, scoring a hat-trick. He went on to spend 18 years at the club, scoring 303 goals, and helping them win three league titles, and reach a European semi-final. He enjoyed further success after moving across the city, winning another league title, and the Scottish Cup.

Midfielder *Michael Stewart*, although born in Edinburgh, joined Manchester United as a teenager, and made eight senior appearances for them, before joining Hearts on loan. It was Hibernian though who signed him on a permanent basis, and he would spend three seasons, with them, before crossing back across the city to join Hearts again.

Interesting facts about the rivalry

- John Robertson of Hearts became known as the "Hammer of Hibs" because he scored 22 goals in 12 seasons at Tynecastle against their great rivals. He is the record scorer in derby matches, followed by Gordon Smith of Hibs, and Bobby Walker of Hearts, who found the net 15 times each.
- Since the Scottish Premier League was founded in 1975, neither club has managed, in a single season, to record a clean sweep. Hearts came the closest in 1996/97 with three wins and a draw.
- For the only time in its history in 1896, the Scottish Cup Final was staged outside Glasgow, Logie Green in Edinburgh the venue.

Fittingly, the two clubs met in the final, Hearts emerging 3 – 1 winners.

- Hearts once went 22 games in a row unbeaten in fixtures between the two, a run that was finally ended by a Gordon Hunter goal at Tynecastle in August 1994.

THE MERSEYSIDE DERBY

LIVERPOOL V EVERTON

Location: Liverpool, England

First Meeting: 13 October 1894

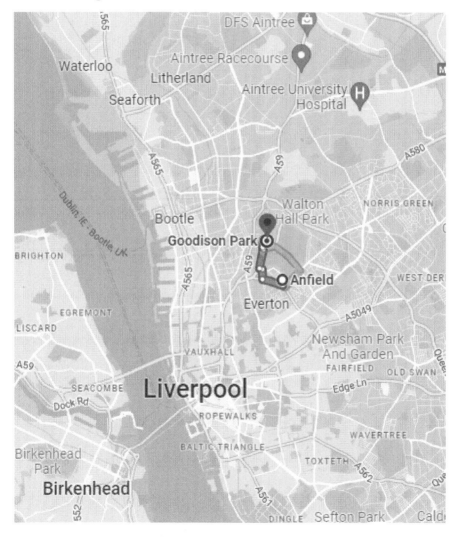

The Merseyside derby is amongst the longest running rivalries, not just in English, but in world football, with the first match between the two clubs played as far back in the 1893 – 94 season. In fact, the relationship goes even further back than that, in the sense that it was Everton who helped give birth to Liverpool in the first place.

Whilst it is fiercely contested on the pitch, relations between the two sets of fans are generally more cordial off it, mainly because they will often share the same school, office, factory or even family.

That does not mean there is not a good deal of teasing and taunting on the derby day. But it seldom deteriorates into the violence that characterises other such encounters.

The origins of the rivalry

Everton were founded in 1978 by members of a Methodist Chapel in the city of Liverpool. They were founding members of the Football League and won their first league title in the 1890 – 91 season.

Originally they played their home games at Anfield, but then a dispute about the rent arose between the Everton committee and club president John Houlding, who owned the land on which Anfield was built. Eventually Everton moved to a new ground at Goodison Park, whilst Houlding formed a new club which became Liverpool with a number of players moving from Everton to join him.

The two grounds are approximately 1,000 metres from each other, separated by Stanley Park, although Everton is not actually in Everton, but in the neighbouring district of Walton.

Unlike many other rivalries, there are no social, economic, political or religious differences which propel somebody to support Liverpool over Everton or vice versa. And, whilst support may be passed down in families, there are plenty of families in Liverpool that house fans of both clubs under the same roof.

It is often called the "friendly derby" because fans have been known to stick together, and it is not marred by the same mutual antipathy that characterises relations between Liverpool and Manchester United fans, for example.

In part this has to do with the history and culture of the city of Liverpool and the tendency of the people who live there to form a united front to the outside world.

Noticeable incidents

Sandy Brown scored one of the finest headed goals in derby history at Goodison Park in 1969. Unfortunately for him, his diving effort was at the wrong end and gave goalkeeper Gordon West no chance. Everton, though, had the last laugh as they equalled Liverpool's seven league title tally at the end of the season.

An otherwise tepid goalless draw in 2000 was illuminated by controversy in injury time. Liverpool pumped a free-kick into the Everton box as they searched for winner, and a clearance hit the back of Everton midfielder Don Hutchinson and deflected past his own keeper. Referee Graham Poll ruled the goal out, though, because he had already blown the full-time whistle.

Liverpool striker Robbie Fowler's goal celebrations in April 1999 landed him in hot water with the authorities. After being subjected to taunts from Everton fans that he had been taking drugs, Fowler scored two goals and then pretended to snort cocaine on the touchline.

The FA did not see the funny side. He was banned for four matches and fined £32,000.

Before the derby in October 2012, Everton manager David Moyes accused Liverpool striker Luis Suárez of being a diver. The Uruguayan responded by setting up Liverpool's opener, and then running towards Moyes in the Everton dug-out and diving in front of him.

Most famous matches

Liverpool 3 – 1 Everton 1 (May 1986)

The two teams met for the first time in a major final in the FA Cup in 1986 at Wembley. Gary Lineker gave Everton the lead, but Liverpool won it with three second-half goals.

Liverpool 3 – 2 Everton (May 1989)

Three years later the two met again in another FA Cup final but it was overshadowed by events at Hillsborough. Twice Liverpool led, only for Stuart McCall to equalise each time. But Ian Rush scored a late winner.

Everton 4 – 4 Liverpool (February 1991)

This FA Cup replay had almost everything, with Liverpool taking the lead four times only to be pegged back each time. Everton would win the second replay.

Everton 2 – 3 Liverpool (April 2001)

This Premier League game saw five goals, a missed penalty, 12 bookings and one red card and was decided in the most audacious manner. Gary McAllister's 44 yard free kick caught Paul Gerrard in the Everton goal napping as he was beaten at his near post.

Crossing the divide

Given the general friendliness between the two clubs there is generally not the same opprobrium when players appear for both clubs in their careers.

They have even had two managers in common. *William Barclay* defected from Everton in 1892, when they moved to Goodison Park, instead opting to join the newly formed Liverpool.

And then at the start of the 2021- 2022 season, *Rafa Benitez* was appointed manager of Everton, having formerly guided Liverpool to Champions League success in 2005. It was never going to work because Everton fans had never forgiven the Spaniard for describing them as a small club during his time at Anfield. He was sacked six months into his tenure.

Other players have enjoyed better fortunes, including *Peter Beardsley, Steve McMahon and Gary Ablett.*

And Jamie Carragher, who spent his entire club career with Liverpool, making more than 700 appearances for them, grew up supporting Everton.

Interesting facts about the rivalry

- In the Premier League era, no other fixture has seen more red cards. The most dismissals in a single game was in 1999 when

Sander Westerveld and Steven Gerrard were sent off for Liverpool, and Francis Jeffers got his marching orders for Everton.

- Although the county of Merseyside was not established until the mid-1970s, the term "Merseyside" side derby pre-dated that by 20 years at least.

- It has also been known as the City of Liverpool derby, and the Lancaster derby.

- Everton fans have become as passionate about seeking justice for the victims of the Hillsborough tragedy as their counterparts from Liverpool. They too lost friends and, in some cases, loved ones in the disaster, and felt as wronged by the smear campaign directed against the city by the British government.

THE SOWETO DERBY

KAIZER CHIEFS V ORLANDO PIRATES

Location: Soweto, Johannesburg, South Africa

First Meeting: 24 January 1970

While rugby is the most popular sport among white South Africans, and, therefore, held sway during the apartheid era, for the vast majority of the rest of the country, football has always been the most followed and supported sport.

And no game excites the passion more than that between the Kaizer Chiefs and Orlando pirates. Wherever and whenever they meet, large crowds can be guaranteed and so can the trouble and violence.

The fixture is no stranger to tragedy over the years, but in a country that has one of the highest homicide rates in the world, many fans accept the risk that comes with attending a game as an occupational hazard.

The origins of the rivalry

The origins of the rivalry can be traced back to the formation of the Chiefs themselves back in 1970.

Kaizer Motaung had begun playing professional football with the Pirates at the age of 16, but in 1968, he crossed the Atlantic to play for Atlanta Chiefs in the (now defunct) North American Soccer League.

He returned to South Africa in 1970, only to find that the Pirates were riven by internal in-fighting and politics. Instead he decided to form his own club to which he lent his name. Despite early opposition he managed to assemble a side made up of a mixture of veterans and talented younger players, and they soon became a force to be reckoned with and attracted a large following.

Unlike many derbies, there are no clear social, political, religious or economic reasons why people from Soweto will support one club or the other. Indeed, there are many cases of divided families, where brothers or sisters will not talk to each other in the run-up to derby day.

For a brief period of time the two clubs found common cause when they helped in the transition from the dual apartheid National Soccer League and National Professional Soccer Leagues to the present Premier Soccer League.

But old rivalries and differences soon re-asserted themselves, and today, every match between them is a grudge match.

Notable Incidents

Sadly, the two biggest sporting tragedies in the history of South African sport have both occurred in Soweto derby matches.

In 1991, the two clubs were playing a pre-season friendly in the town of Orkney, located 120 miles to the North-West of Johannesburg.

Although the stadium had an official capacity of only 23,000 people, due to a failure of stewarding and police control, more than 30,000 crowded into the ground and there was no segregation between the two sets of supporters.

When the Chiefs scored in controversial fashion and the referee upheld the goal, supporters from the Pirates objected. Some threw cans and fruit at their opposite numbers whilst a group armed with knives began attacking Chiefs' supporters.

Innocent bystanders attempting to flee the violence were trampled underfoot, or crushed to death against riot-control fences. 42 people died due to asphyxia related injuries and scores more were injured.

A decade later there was a repeat, this time at the Ellis Park Stadium in Johannesburg.

Again there was a case of overcrowding, with more than 100,000 people trying to gain entrance to a ground designed with a capacity of 60,000.

The Chiefs scored first, but when the Pirates equalised, the crowd spilled forward trying to get a glimpse of the action, and, as they spilled forward and into the press boxes, a deadly crush ensued.

43 people died and scores were injured. It was later alleged that untrained security staff had made the situation worse by firing tear gas at the stampeding fans, although this version of events was later denied by the South African Police Service.

More recently, in 2017 two people were killed and several others injured during a stampede at the FNB stadium in Soweto caused by people trying to sell or present fake tickets at one of the gates into the ground.

Most famous matches

Kaizer Chiefs 7 – 3 Orlando Pirates (1972)

The highest aggregate number of goals scored in the history of the fixture, and the joint highest winning margin as well equalled again by the Chief's 5 – 1 win in 1975, and the same score line, except for the Pirates dominating in 1990.

Kaizer Chiefs 1 – 3 Orlando Pirates (November 2010)

In the late 2010s, the Pirates dominated games between the two, and the start of that era can be traced to this match, when they out-classed their opponents.

Orlando Pirates 3 – 2 Kaizer Chiefs (March 2012)

One of South Africa's most famous football exports, Benny McCarthy played in his first Soweto derby in 2012 after spells abroad with the likes of Ajax, Porto, Blackburn Rovers and West Ham. And he marked the occasion by opening the scoring as Pirates ran put 3 – 2 winners.

Kaizer Chiefs 3 – 2 Orlando Pirates (November 2019)

What had seemed a comfortable day at the office for the Chiefs as they took an early two goals lead soon turned anything but when the Pirates stormed back to equalise. A late penalty from Daniel Cardoso, though, sent the Chiefs' fans home happy.

Crossing the divide

Apart from *Kaizer Motaung*, the former Pirates player, whose decision to found his own club began the rivalry in the first place there have been a large number of players who have appeared for both sides.

Gabriel Khoza, Blessing Mgidi, Jerry Sadike, Donald "Ace" Khuse, Marks Maponyane and *Marc Batchelor* have all scored wearing the colours of both clubs in derby games.

Meanwhile, *Kosta Papić, Walter da Silva, Ted Dumitru, Augusto Palacios, Joe Frickleton,* and *Vladimir Vermezović* have both managed the two Soweto sides.

Interesting facts about the rivalry

- Percy "Chippa" Moloi of the Pirates has the distinction of being the first man to score in a derby in 1970.
- Alfred 'Russia" Jacobs of the Pirates and Fani Madida of the Chiefs share the record for having scored in four successive derbies. Jacobs managed the feat between 1970 and 1971, and Madida between 1991 and 1992.
- Goalkeeper Joseph 'Banks" Sethodi of the Chiefs scored penalties in three successive derbies in 1972. He had also found the net from the spot the previous year.
- Namibian born Herman Blaschke was the first foreigner to score in the derby.

O Clássico

BENFICA V PORTO

Location: Portugal

First Meeting: Porto 2–8 Benfica

Although Portugal has a number of derbies, arguably the most intense and closely fought is that between Benfica and Porto. Its origins can be traced back to the fact that the two clubs come from the two largest cities in Portugal, Lisbon and Porto, and also stem from the country's political, cultural and social history.

Between them, the two clubs have won more trophies than any other club in Portuguese history and comprise two of the "Big Three", Sporting being the other one. However, it is usually the matches between the two that decide the destiny of most major domestic trophies.

The origins of the rivalry

The origins consist of the differences between Lisbon and Porto. Lisbon, the capital, is in the south of the country, whose inhabitants are considered wealthier, more powerful, and laidback than those from the industrial and hardworking north, epitomised by the major port and trading city of Porto.

The two regions co-exist and compete with each other in almost every area of public life.

A famous Portuguese saying is "In Porto they work, in Lisbon they spend." For those in Porto there is a sense that the Lisbon is overprotected and that it has privileges that it does not deserve. And there is also the sense of being patronised and disadvantaged by the capital that many living in the provinces in European countries feel.

The people from Lisbon are known as 'alfacinhas" (little lettuces) whilst their Porto counterparts are the "tripeiros" (the tripe-eaters). A real clash of cultures and styles!

Porto were founded in 1893, Benfica 11 years later, with the pair first meeting in a friendly in 1912. Benfica won that match 8 -2, and Porto would have to wait eight years until their first O Clássico victory.

In the early years there was no real animosity between the two sides, although things began to change in the 1930s when the two clubs began to compete in official competitions, and often found themselves going head to head for the top prizes.

However, in the next three decades, Porto went into decline as the City of Lisbon dominated Portugal football – Benfica, Sporting and even Belenenses winning league titles.

Porto's revival came in the late 1970s with the arrival of Jorge Nuno Pinto da Costa and Jose Maria Pedroto as director and coach respectively, whose primary motivation was to beat Lisbon at all costs.

Pedroto coined the phrase "a trophy won by Porto is worth twice or more than those from Lisbon teams". The pair deliberately cultivated a confrontational attitude, and Porto gradually assumed ascendancy, and became the most successful team in the country after the April 25 Carnation Revolution in 1974 when democracy was re-established in Portugal.

Today, matches between the two are the most eagerly awaited in Portugal, and will be amongst the most watched even by neutral fans.

Notable incidents

Both clubs operate other sports under their umbrella, and basketball, hockey, handball and futsal matches between the two have seen confrontations between fans and amongst players. In 2012, for example, when Benfica beat Porto to win their 23rd league basketball title, they could only receive the trophy in the locker room because they were held there for two hours whilst the police struggled to restore order between fighting fans.

Now 84, Pinto da Costa remains president of Porto, despite being accused and cleared of corruption charges. Despite having won the most titles as club president, he has not softened his attitude to Lisbon in the slightest. When an executive for one of Portugal's main electricity operators explained to him in 2013 why Benfica winning the title would boost the GDP of the Portuguese economy, he told him Porto would be looking for another electricity supplier.

More recently, a match featuring the junior squads of both teams spiralled out of control when players from both sides squared up, and then some of the Benfica players tried to get into the stands to fight with Porto supporters who had been heckling them.

Most famous matches

Benfica 2 – 1 Porto (May 2004)

In 2004 the two sides met in the final of the Portuguese Cup, with Porto chasing the treble, having also won the Champions League and Primeira League. An extra-time winner from Benfica was to deny them, however.

Porto 5 – 0 Benfica (November 2010)

This was Porto's biggest ever home win over their rivals and one that is still celebrated to this day.

Porto 2 – 1 Benfica (May 2013)

Some have described this as the best "O Clássico" match of all time, and one of the most significant. The two sides met in the penultimate game of the season level on points at the top, but with Benfica having a slightly better goal difference. The away team just needed a point to virtually guarantee the title, but instead it was their rivals who claimed the spoils.

Crossing the divide

Unlike with some rivalries, there have been a number of players and managers, who have spent time with both clubs. The best known of these managers are *Béla Guttmann* and *Jose Mourinho*. Although Guttmann is remembered as the man who guided Benfica to European Cup success in 1961 and 1962, he had a season in charge at Porto before moving to Lisbon.

And Mourinho had a brief stint at Benfica before leading Porto to Champions League success, which opened the door for him to Chelsea and the appointments which have followed.

In terms of players the best known include former Portuguese international striker *Paolo Futré*, the Uruguayan right-back *Maxi Pereira* and Argentine defender *Nicolàs Otamendi*, who Premier League fans will remember from his spell with Manchester City.

Interesting facts about the rivalry

- In 2018 five people including the head of Benfica's legal department and a computer operator at the Portuguese Justice

Ministry were arrested on corruption charges involving Benfica. There is strong evidence that the authorities were tipped off by an email sent by somebody affiliated with Porto.

- For years there were suspicions that rivalry between Porto and Benfica players affected the performance of the Portuguese national team. Benfica players used to sit in the front on the team bus, Porto players in the middle and those from Sporting in the back.

- Although the term O Clássico is generally reserved for matches between these two clubs, it can also be used generically to describe any big game in Portugal.

THE ETERNAL DERBY

RED STAR BELGRADE V PARTIZAN BELGRADE

Location: Belgrade, Serbia

First Meeting: 5 January 1947

Both Red Star and Partizan Belgrade were formed in the aftermath of the Second World War in the country that became known as Yugoslavia, although they are now in Serbia.

Since the break-up of Yugoslavia, the teams have dominated Serbian football to the extent that the only time their joint stranglehold on the title was broken was back in 1998 when it went to FK Obilic in controversial circumstances (the career criminal and paramilitary leader Željko Ražnatović also known as Arkan had taken over the club and threatened players on opposing teams with dire consequences if they scored against them).

Even in the old days of the Yugoslav league which was more competitive, the two Belgrade teams were the most successful in the competition, Red Star claiming 19, and Partizan 11 titles.

Today, matches between the two have become an attraction for tourists, who want to experience the spectacle of packed stadiums, flares, fireworks and chants.

The threat of violence, though, is never far from the surface, with both clubs having notorious group or "ultra" fan groups, who have been known to fight among themselves.

Nor is the rivalry confined to just football, Basketball matches between their two affiliated clubs are some of the most intense in Europe.

The origins of the rivalry

Red Star were instigated by the Communist Party of Yugoslavia, whilst, six months' later Partizan were created by the Yugoslav People's Army, the two groups competing for power and influence in the government of Josep Tito. The grounds are just 400 yards apart and are separated by a park which has numerous small hills and clumps of trees which provides warring gangs with cover, thus, proximity as much as political affiliations created a rivalry almost from the start.

Although they represented different factions, for a while in the early 1990s there was common ground between them, as Serbians identified with the two clubs, as Yugoslavia fragmented into different republics as a bloody civil war broke out.

In fact, some point to a match in 1990 between Red Star and Dinamo Zagreb as the start of the Croatian War of independence, and the more extreme elements of both fan bases, particularly Red Star's would take part in the armed conflicts that were to follow as members of various militia groups.

In reality, the rivalry between Red Star and Partizan has more to do with the enmity between the two sets of supporters, with football very much secondary.

And whilst Red Star have always been regarded as the team of Serb nationalism, in reality Partizan fans are scarcely less patriotic.

Red Star's Ultras are known as Delije (Heroes), although the term was not officially recognised until 1989. The Delije are composed of four main sub-groups, as well as numerous other smaller factions. Whilst in-fighting among them is not uncommon, they tend to present a united front on derby day.

Meanwhile Partizan have their Grobari (grave diggers). The name was originally bestowed on them disparagingly by Red Star fans because Partizan play in black and white colours, but then the Partizan ultras willingly embraced it.

Noticeable incidents

A match between the two teams in April 2015 was marred by crowd violence which saw the kick-off delayed. 35 police officers were injured, and 41 fans were arrested, including some who threw stun grenades at law enforcement officials inside the stadium. Meanwhile, a van was stopped headed to the ground loaded with bricks and rocks intended to be used as missiles.

In 2017, a mass brawl between supporters during a derby match left at least 17 people needing hospital treatment. Police were forced to intervene to end the clashes, as the hooligan problems which have beset matches between the two, reappeared.

Most famous matches

Partizan 3 – 4 Red Star (January 1947)

This was the inaugural match between the two rivals and ended in a victory for the red half of Belgrade. Partizan won the reverse fixture by a single goal, kick-starting the rivalry.

Red Star 3 - 0 Partizan (May 1948)

Red Star had never won a major trophy before this match and began the game as underdogs. However, they broke their duck winning the Yugoslav Cup against their fiercest rivals, with a triumph their fans celebrated for years.

Red Star 2 – 3 Partizan (May 1992) (aggregate score of two legged Yugoslav Cup)

Red Star were the dominant team in the league that year, yet, against all the odds, Partizan beat them in the away leg, and held them to a draw in the reverse fixture. It was their first trophy since 1989 and heralded a successful era for them, as they added seven more domestic trophies in the decade that followed.

Crossing the divide

Given the hatred that exists between the two clubs, relatively few players have dared to switch allegiance. There have been transfers between the two clubs but none since 2009.

Here are a few who dared to make the switch

Velibor Vasović

Defender Vasović made his debut for Partizan in 1958, and would go on to play for them for five seasons, before signing for their arch rivals. However, his stay at Red Star lasted just six months, during which time he and his family were the subject of death threats.

He returned to Partizan at the beginning of the 1964 season, before securing a move to Ajax where he became their first foreign captain.

Goran Milojević

Attacking midfielder Milojević came through the youth ranks at Red Star and went on to make 98 appearances for the senior team, before moving across the city. He would then turn out for Partizan 59 times, before moving abroad to play in France, Spain and Mexico.

Cléo

Brazilian striker Cléo, who later became a naturalised Serbian, was the last player to move between the clubs where money changed hands. He joined Red Star on loan from a Portuguese club, scoring 8 goals in 20 appearances, and then was signed by Partizan the following season. He scored better than one goal every two games in the black and white shirt.

Interesting facts about the rivalry

- Both clubs have suffered from severe financial problems in the past two decades. Red Star were suspended from the Champions League for the 2014-15 season over unpaid debts, whilst several years later, Partizan almost faced an extended UEFA ban for breaching FFP (Financial Fair Play Regulations) for the third time in five years.
- Although Red Star is the Anglicised name of the team and the one by which they are generally known in Europe, nowadays they are locally called Crvena Zvezda.
- Belgrade locals call the police who are deployed on derby day in mass numbers "turtles" because of the amount of protective clothing that they wear.

LE CLASSIQUE

PARIS SAINT-GERMAIN V OLYMPIQUE DE MARSEILLE

Location: France

First Meeting: 12 December 1971

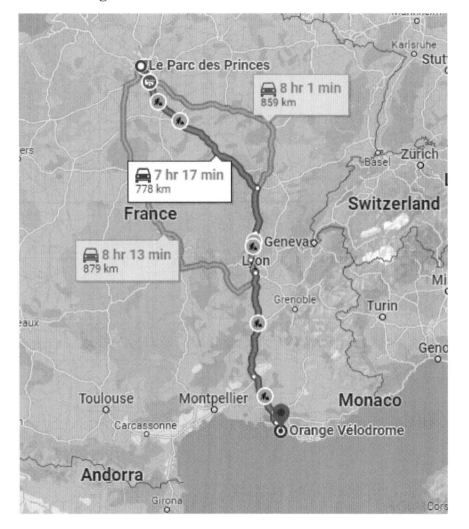

Although the rivalry between Paris Saint-Germain (PSG) and Olympique Marseille (OM) is comparatively recent as compared to many other such match-ups, that does not make it any less intense. In fact, it reflects divisions in France that stretch back centuries, between the two largest cities in the country, and the old enmity between the North and the South, the Capital versus the Provinces.

Derby matches (Le Classique as it is known) are the most watched in the country, not least because both clubs have wide followings throughout France. Added impetus to the animosity between the two clubs has been the takeover of PSG by wealthy Qatari owners, which has enabled them to acquire a team full of superstars like Kylian Mbappé, Neymar, and Lionel Messi.

That has added envy to the list of ingredients, not just from Marseille supporters, but from fans of every other club in France.

The origins of the rivalry

OM were founded in 1899 and were already one of the most successful clubs in France by the time PSG came into existence 71 years later. However, by the 1960s Marseille had declined so much that they were almost an irrelevance. Crowds dwindled to the extent that one French Cup tie in 1965 attracted just 434 paying supporters.

At that point Marcel Leclerc, the owner of a media group, stepped in and used his wealth to become a team that would become one of the most exciting in European football.

Meanwhile, Paris retained its status as the only major European capital without a major football team. That was until a group of ambitious businessmen got together and merged several smaller clubs into what would become PSG.

With the two cities nearly 500 miles apart, initial games between the two clubs were relatively low key, but that began to change as they increasingly started competing against each other for major domestic honours.

And it also came to signify something deeper and more primeval in French society. Many French people resent Paris for its economic, cultural and political dominance. It is also believed that some Parisians tend to look down on those from the provinces, especially those from the south.

Most recently, PSG have become representative of new found wealth and of foreign investment, whilst Marseille have positioned themselves as the club of the people – conveniently failing to recall that they have had their own share of wealthy owners, among them Bernard Tapie, who had to resign after a match fixing scandal.

Currently the visiting fans for derby matches are heavily constricted in an attempt to avoid violence, although that does not stop rival fans clashing in neutral venues.

Notable incidents

A mid-table OM thrashed PSG, who were title hopefuls, in October 2000, in a match that saw former PSG team mates Laurent Leroy and Jerôme Leroy dismissed after coming to blows. Florian Maurice scored a late goal for OM and celebrated by taking off his right boot, and throwing it into the crowd.

Two hours before kick-off in the fixture between the two sides in October 2005, there was a smell of ammonia in the PSG dressing room. OM then used further destabilisation tactics by getting a well-known porn star, who was also a Marseille fan, to parade past whilst the PSG players were changing.

In 2010 one PSG fan was left in a coma and subsequently died following a clash between the capital club's two main support groups – the Boulogne Boys and the Supras Auteuil – following a 3 – 0 loss to OM. 15 fans were arrested and a ban on travelling support was initiated.

In September 2020, shortly after PSG lost in the final of the Champions League to Bayern Munich came a match dubbed "The Battle of Paris." In injury time a mass brawl broke out on the pitch, and four players were sent off. Neymar accused one of the OM players of making a racist comment as he left the pitch, but he in turn was alleged to have issued a homophobic slur. The referee showed 19 cards in total, a record for a French league fixture, whilst Neymar became the first player in French football to pick up two red cards in the same game.

Most famous matches

PSG 4 – 3 Marseille (April 1979)

This remains the highest scoring fixture between the two clubs, and was decided by a late winner from Carlos Bianchi who scored with a long range shot.

Marseille 1 – 0 PSG (October 1989)

Arguably the one game that kick started the rivalry more than any other. Both teams went into the match knowing that a win would put them into prime position to win the league title that year. More spice was added by PSG president Francis Borelli as he accused his counterpart Bernard Tapie of match fixing.

Marseille won it and effectively sealed their first title in 17 years.

PSG 1 - 2 Marseille (May 1997)

After Marseille had been demoted to Ligue 2 following a bribery scandal their first match back in the top flight against their rivals meant they travelled to Paris with a point to prove. And win they did, although even today there are PSG fans who believe that Fabrizio Ravanelli dived for the penalty that eventually proved decisive.

Marseille 2 - 4 PSG (May 2016)

In 2016 the two met in the French Cup final before a record crowd of 80,000 spectators. Zlatan Ibrahimović, playing in his last game for PSG, scored two and assisted another, as PSG won the trophy for a tenth successive year.

Crossing the divide

A number of players have represented both clubs over the years. Here are some of the most prominent.

Gabriel Heinze

A name familiar to Manchester United fans, the Argentine defender joined PSG from Real Valladolid in Spain in 2001. He would play 105 games for the club before his switch to Old Trafford three years later. He returned to France five years later with OM despite swearing previously he would never play for them. During his time at Manchester United, he also tried to force a move to Liverpool after being disillusioned with their manager Sir Alex Ferguson.

Lassana Diarra

Diarra was a much travelled midfielder who played for clubs in England, Spain and Russia in his career before returning to France and OM. He appeared in 45 games and briefly captained them, before being released when he joined PSG, going on to win a Ligue 1 title in his time with them.

Claude Makélélé

Makélélé was the defensive midfielder who came to define the position in his time at Real Madrid and then in Jose Mourinho's first spell at Chelsea. Before then he had already played for OM for one season, and later played for their rivals in the tail-end of his career.

George Weah

Weah, who is now President of Liberia, is the only African player to win the Ballon D'Or. During his time in Paris he won two French Cups, the league title, and the League Cup, before heading to Italy and AC Milan, where he would enjoy even more success. He then later had a short spell in Marseille, scoring five goals in 20 appearances.

Interesting facts about the rivalry

- They are the only two major French teams to win European silverware. PSG lifted the UEFA Cup Winners Cup in 1996, and OM the Champions League in 1993.
- Marseille are the most supported club in France, followed by PSG.
- An alternative theory about the rivalry is that it is artificially created, by Bernard Tapie, the owner of OM at the time and the media group Canal+ which had just acquired PSG. By making up the rivalry, the aim was to gain more subscribers to the newly launched satellite broadcaster.

THE DERBY OF THE ETERNAL RIVALS

OLYMPIACOS V PANATHINAIKOS

Location: Athens/Piraeus, Greece

First Meeting: 28 June 1925

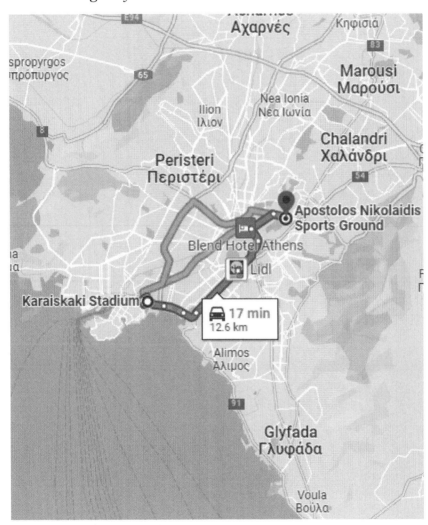

Olympiacos and Panathinaikos are the two most successful clubs in the history of Greece, and the rivalry between the two clubs and sets of fans is intense. As with many derbies its origins owe much to the social and economic divisions between different classes and neighbourhoods in Athens and the surrounding areas, although today, the fanbases of both clubs are drawn from all strata of Greek society.

However, derbies between the two are always fraught occasions, and there have been numerous fan clashes over the years, riots, and sadly the occasional deaths. No wonder that the derby is sometimes known as the "Mother of All Battles."

The origins of the rivalry

The origins can be traced back to modern Greece which gained its independence from the Ottoman Empire in 1821. In 1832 Athens was declared the capital of the new nation, whilst nearby Piraeus, which had been a deserted city, evolved to become a major port and population centre. In fact, so great was the number of Greek refugees flooding into the city that it gradually became absorbed within the boundaries of Athens again.

Panathinaikos was the first to be formed in 1908 and were from the centre of Athens, and were considered the representatives of the higher or patrician class of Greek society. Olympiacos were not established until 17 years later, and being based in Piraeus, from the outset positioned themselves as the club of the working man.

When Olympiacos enjoyed early success, it provided a way for the people of Piraeus to contempt for the wealthier classes in Athens who tended to look down on them. In addition, the club began to attract fans from the rest of Greece who believed themselves to be victims of social and economic unfairness, and resented the power of the capital and the governing elite.

Although the class differences between the two clubs may have been eroded in time, the animosity between the two sets of fans remains undiminished. With both clubs having large sets of fanbases that follow them at home and abroad, hooliganism has become a common phenomenon in matches involving them.

Neutrals know that it is best to avoid the area when one club is hosting another.

Notable incidents

In 2007 a 22-year old Panathinaikos fan Mihalis Filopoulos was stabbed to death in a town close to Athens where a women's volleyball game between the two clubs was scheduled to take place. Hooligans from both clubs had pre-arranged to meet there. In the subsequent fall-out and national outrage a police investigation was launched into organised supporters groups, and the outcome was a two week suspension on all team sporting events in Greece.

In November 2015 a derby match was called off as fans fought with riot police. Olympiacos striker Alfred Finnbogason was hit by a flare as he walked on to the pitch, and with the violence continuing, the referee called the match off after just 30 minutes. That was the signal for broken chairs and advertising hoardings to litter the pitch, and missiles were thrown at the police.

Olympiacos fans were not even in the stadium because visiting fans were banned in the Greek Super League. That though, did not stop them clashing with their opposite numbers before and after the match.

Nearly four years later another derby was abandoned in similar circumstances. In a bid to ensure neutrality in a country where allegations of corruption in football are endemic, German referee Marco Fritz was appointed to officiate the match in March 2019.

The match was interrupted as early as the fifth minute when a few fans invaded the pitch, but the security situation continued to deteriorate, and clashes broke out all over the stadium between rival groups of fans and riot police.

Fritz ordered the players back to the dressing room and called for the stadium to be evacuated so the game could continue. But one hour later, when he observed there were still fans present, he called off the game. The match was awarded to Olympiacos, and Panathinaikos were hit with a points deduction and a heavy fine.

Most famous matches

Olympiacos 3 – 4 Panathinaikos (February 1990)

One of the highest scoring match in derby history was marred by scuffles among fans, a pitch invasion by officials from both clubs, a temporary walk-out by the referee, and then further fighting in the stands.

Panathinaikos 0 – 2 Olympiacos (April 1997)

Olympiacos went to the home of their hated rivals, and their victory went a long way to sealing the league title that season. It is also widely seen as the catalyst for their subsequent domination of Greek football which continues to this day.

Panathinaikos 3 – 1 Olympiacos (May 2004)

The two sides met in the Greek Cup final with Panathinaikos having already wrapped up an increasingly rare league title. On the eve of the match Panathinaikos were stunned by the news that striker Antonis Nikopolidis intended to leave them for their hated rivals. They responded by leaving him out of their squad altogether, and his deputy Kostas Chalkias went on to have a fine game which the green and white team thoroughly dominated.

Olympiacos 2 – 1 Panathinaikos (February 2011)

This game is best remembered for the actions of home team's captain Vasilis Torosidis, who was sent off and subsequently banned for five matches after head butting an opponent. The aftermath of the game saw a pitch invasion by Olympiacos fans, numerous arrests, and a one match stadium ban for Olympiacos supporters.

Crossing the divide

Unlike maby rivalries, it has been fairly common over the years for players to switch from one club to another. They have even had five managers in common – *Stjepan Bobek, Lakis Petropoulos, Helmut Senekowitsch,* and the Polish pair of *Kazimierz Gorski,* and *Jacek Gmoch.*

Among the best known players to make the short journey are:

Antonis Antoniadis

Nicknamed "The Tall" because of his height, Antoniadis started his career being used as a goalkeeper, before he found his true position as a striker. With Panathinaikos, he scored 177 goals in 222 appearances, and was the top scorer in the Greek league on five occasions. He then had one season with Olympiacos where he averaged better than one goal every two games.

Nikos Sarganis

Goalkeeper Sarganis spent six seasons with Olympiacos before controversially joining Panathinaikos in the summer of 1985. He was nicknamed "The Phantom" by the Danish press for his exploits in an international playing for Greece in Copenhagen.

Georgios Delikaris

The striker is remembered as one of the greatest players of his generation and was once dubbed the "Greek George Best". Still remembered as an Olympiacos legend, he shocked many when he moved to Panathinaikos where he saw out the last three years of his playing career.

Georgios Georgiadis

Right winger Georgiadis was part of the Panathinaikos team that reached the semi-finals of the Champions League in 1995 – 1996. His form earned him a move to the Premier League with Newcastle United, but he failed to impress, and returned to Greece with PAOK. He moved to Olympiacos in 2003, and spent three seasons with them.

Interesting facts about the rivalry

- Although Olympiacos are the most successful club in Greek domestic football, it is their rivals who have had the greater success on the international stage. Panathinaikos were runners -up in the European Cup in 1971, and won the now defunct Balkans Cup, a tournament contested between clubs from Albania, Bulgaria, Greece, Romania, Turkey, and the former Yugoslavia.
- Panathinaikos and Olympiacos fans are known respectively as 'vazelos" (vassals) and "anchovies". Vassals because Panathinaikos fans traditionally come from the upper social strata who use a kind of gel in their hair which resembles Vaseline. And anchovies

because, in 1965, fans of Olympiacos welcomed their opponents with fish cages which they had taken from the port of Piraeus.

- One game in January 2003 ended 3 – 2 in Panathinaikos with all the goals scored by players of the home team. Panathinaikos took a two goal lead, but then conceded two own goals before scoring a late winner at the right end.

DERBY DELLA CAPITALE

ROMA V LAZIO

Location: Rome, Italy

First Meeting: 8 December 1929

Few fixtures in Italy attract so much hostility and animosity between the fans as the Derby Della Capitale between Lazio and Roma. Separating them is not just a few miles of the capital but a multitude of differences rooted in the Italian history of the 20th century, fascist versus the left wing, the middle and wealthy versus the working class.

The result is a potent mix of resentments, jealousies, and spite, which often sees the matches between the two marred by ugly acts of violence between the Ultra hooligan groups before, during and after matches.

It is no wonder that the hundreds of thousands of tourists that visit Rome each year are warned to avoid the Stadio Olimpico – the ground they share in common – on derby day.

The origins of the rivalry

Lazio are the older of the two, being formed in 1900, although they were then known as Societa Podistica Lazio. In 1904, they played their first match against another side from the Rome area, Virtus, and this is widely considered the first derby.

Roma did not come into existence until 1927, when three local teams, Roman, Alba-Audace, and Fortitudo merged.

The fascist dictator of Italy, Benito Mussolini, himself a keen football fan, wanted to create a single Roman club to compete against the major Northern clubs like Inter and AC Milan, and Juventus. However, one of the most influential supporters of his regime, General Giorgio Vaccaro, was a Lazio supporter, and because they were the only team from Rome who were not part of the merger, they got the government's backing.

That began the long association between Lazio and fascist politics which continues, even to this day. It is no coincidence that Lazio's emblem is the eagle, representing strength and power, which also featured on the flag of the National Fascist Party.

The burgeoning rivalry between the two clubs was also fed by the location they were situated in the city. Lazio fans were mainly from Parioli in the northern part of the city, which is considered to be mainly middle and upper class area. Roma was situated in the working class neighbourhood of Testaccio. As a consequence, a number of their fans are left-leaning when it comes to politics.

Notable incidents

The first death recorded as a result of fan violence occurred in the derby between the two sides in October 1979. 33-year old mechanic Vincenzo Paparelli, a Lazio fan was attending the match with his wife, Wanda, the pair having been given tickets by his brother who could not make it. Paparelli was eating a sandwich before the match when he was struck directly in the left eye by a nautical flare fired by an 18-year old Roma fan. He died at the scene.

In 2004, rumours that a boy had been murdered by police caused a derby match to be stopped after just five minutes. Fighting broke out between both sets of fans, although it was later found that the allegations were untrue, and the boy had been sheltering under a tarpaulin after suffering an anxiety attack. Nevertheless, more than 160 people were injured in the ensuing riot.

Meanwhile, in 2010 a mother and child had a lucky escape when they inadvertently became caught up in clashes between rival fans. The pair happened to drive past the spot where supporters' groups were fighting, when their vehicle was attacked. Fortunately they managed to escape the car before it was engulfed in flames and completely destroyed.

There were more ugly scenes before a derby match in 2013. A number of fans were stabbed, and an ambulance had to be abandoned after fireworks, rocks and sticks were thrown at it. State security was put on high alert and local businesses shut up shop early before more violence occurred.

An illustration of the unpleasantness that attends some derby fixtures came in 2017 when antisemitic stickers of Anne Frank in a Roma jersey were left at the Stadio Olimpico. As a result, a number of Serie A clubs took anti-racist actions, Lazio were among them, but their actions were opposed by some of their fans.

Most famous matches

Lazio 1- 1 Roma (November 1992)

Paul Gascoigne made himself an instant hero to Lazio fans by scoring his first goal for the club, a late equaliser in the derby.

Roma 1 – 0 Lazio (December 2000)

An own goal by Lazio's Paolo Negro gave Roma victory in this match and they went on to win the Scudetto with Lazio finishing third. Even to this day Negro is taunted by home fans for his error.

Lazio 1 – 0 Roma (May 2013)

In 2013 the pair met in the 2013 Coppa Italia final. It was the first cup final involving the pair and was won by a goal from Senad Lulić.

Lazio 2 – 2 Roma (January 2015)

Two goals from Francesco Totto helped his side come from behind to draw this fixture, and, in the process, he became the all-time top scorer in derby fixtures. He celebrated by taking a selfie in front of Roma fans, having given his iPhone to the goalkeeping coach before kick-off.

Crossing the divide

Although it was not unknown for players to have appeared for both the clubs prior to the Second World War, it has been less common in recent years. Among those who have braved the experience are:

Siniša Mihajlović

Mihajlović joined Roma a year after winning the European Cup with Red Star Belgrade and would spend two seasons there, before moving to Sampdoria. He then returned to the capital with Lazio, earning enmity from the Roma faithful who labelled him a traitor.

Diego Fuser

Fuser played for Lazio between 1992 and 1998 and captained the side for a while. He then joined Parma before heading back south again, this time to Roma, although injury restricted his appearances.

Pedro

Spanish and English fans will remember Pedro for his years with Barcelona and then Chelsea. When he left Stamford Bridge he headed to Roma for a season, before falling out with Jose Mourinho, and joining their rivals.

Interesting facts about the rivalry

- The derby between the two has been hosted at five different stadiums over the years, beginning with the Stadio della Rondinella in 1929. Since then, games have taken place at Campo Testaccio, the Stadio Nazionale, the Stadio Flaminio, and, most recently, the Stadio Olimpico.
- Since the year 2000, no other fixture in the top five leagues in Europe has produced more red cards. Lazio midfielder Cristian Ledesma was sent off three times during his time in Rome, whilst former Roma captain Danielle de Rossi racked up more bookings than any other player.
- After he retired de Rossi fulfilled a long held ambition to watch a derby match as a fan, employing the help of a professional make-up artist and donning a wig, false nose and glasses so that he would not be recognised.
- In January 2021 the two teams played on a Friday for the first time. It was the only day of the week that the fixture had never been scheduled before.

THE MANCHESTER DERBY

MANCHESTER CITY V MANCHESTER UNITED

Location: Manchester, England

First Meeting: 12 November 1881

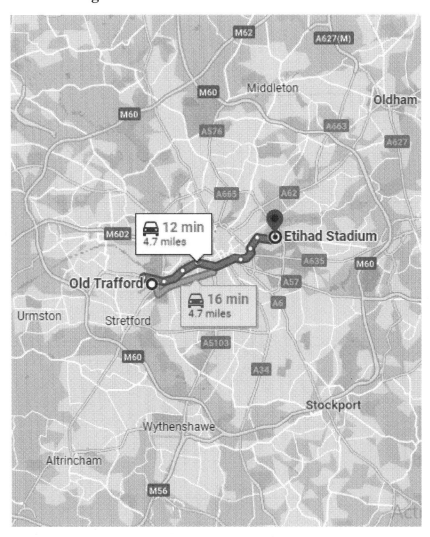

Although the first meeting between Manchester United and Manchester City took place in 1881, for a time there was nothing special about the rivalry between the two teams, and, before the Second World War, it was not uncommon for football fans in the Manchester area to watch United one week and City the next.

Attitudes later hardened and, as hooliganism began to affect the British football, derby matches became more and more bad tempered both on and off the field.

However, with the two clubs often not even playing in the same division, it took until a substantial injection of wealth into City for the rivalry to reach a new level.

The origins of the rivalry

The teams first met in 1881, although under different names. St. Marks (West Gorton), who would later become City, hosted Newton Heath (who would eventually become United).

Initially they were two teams among many in the Manchester area, but they both grew in size and stature so that by 1890s, they were regarded as the biggest clubs in the city.

In the early 20th century, when a financial scandal involving City saw 17 players suspended, a number of City players subsequently joined United and helped them win their first league title. At the time, such moves were welcomed as helping a fellow Manchester club.

Relations between the two clubs remained mainly cordial before the Second World War, and many fans would watch both clubs when they were at home.

Even when things became more fractious, the comparative lack of success for City and the fact that they spent almost a decade outside the top flight of English football meant that they were not taken seriously by United fans, who instead looked to Liverpool as the team they most wanted to beat.

The rivalry took on a new impetus when City were bought in 2008 by Sheikh Mansour bin Zayed bin Sultan Al Nahyan through an Abu Dhabi investment group. Suddenly they were catapulted into a big club in terms of financial investment in both playing staff and facilities, and began to flex their new found muscle both on and off the pitch.

That led Alex Ferguson, the United manager at the time, to brand them as "noisy neighbours". The Scot, who never shied away from mind games, meant it as an insult, implying that City, for all their new found wealth, were a small club and did not have the same history of winning silverware as United.

Manchester United fans agreed with his sentiments, but City supporters took it as a proof of United's arrogance.

Since Ferguson's retirement, it is City who have emerged as the dominant football force in Manchester, and now it is they who taunt their cross-town rivals.

Notable incidents

In December 1970 a tackle by George Best broke the leg of City's Glyn Pardoe and so severe was the injury, that amputation was considered at one point. The following season Francis Lee of City accused Best of diving during a game, and threw himself theatrically to the floor to illustrate his point.

Denis Law, although regarded as a United legend, had two spells with Manchester City, with a spell in Italy with Torino and at Old Trafford in the middle.

During his 11 years at Old Trafford he scored 171 goals in 309 appearances, and formed part of a legendary front three with Bobby Charlton and George Best also known as the 'Holy Trinity' by Manchester United faithful. He was then offered a contract by Manchester City for the 1973 – 1974 season and, in what would prove to be his final game in professional football, he scored a backheel goal that condemned United to relegation. A number of pitch invasions by United fans followed, and a disconsolate Law, who refused to celebrate the goal, was substituted and left the pitch with his head down.

In April 2001 a long-standing feud between United captain Roy Keane and Alf-Inge Haaland reached its culmination. Three years earlier Keane suffered an ACL injury following a tackle by Haaland who was playing for

Leeds at the time. As Keane lay on the ground, Haaland accused him of feigning injury.

The Irishman never forgot or forgave and received a red card for a knee-high tackle on Haaland. In his later autobiography, he admitted that he had deliberately set out to injure the Norwegian. He was fined £150,000 and given a five match ban.

Mario Balotelli's period with City was controversial, with stories of frequent bust-ups with team mates, and a wild array of other allegations, most of which were fabricated, although he did admit to letting off fireworks in his house, causing the curtains to catch fire. That earned him a "bad boy reputation" which he referenced by wearing a t-shirt under his jersey bearing the words "Why Always me?" He revealed it when he opened the scoring in the derby in October 2011, and his side went on to win the match 6 – 1.

Most famous matches

Manchester City 5 – 1 Manchester United (September 1989)

Having been out of the First Division for two years, City celebrated their return in style with a thumping win over their neighbours which gave their fans temporary bragging rights.

Manchester City 2 – 3 Manchester United (November 1993)

City taunted United fans with the fact they had been knocked out of the Champions League four days earlier and had even more to cheer about when they went two nil up at half-time. An Eric Cantona inspired comeback though soon shut them up.

Manchester United 1 – 6 Manchester City (October 2011)

Ferguson did not have many bad days in charge of United, but he would label this thrashing at home as his "worst ever". It was only 1 – 0 at half-time but a red card for United proved catastrophic as City were rampant.

Manchester City 2 – 3 Manchester United (April 2018)

City were 13 points clear at the top of the Premier League table and a win on home soil against their big rivals would have sealed the title. All was going to plan at half-time as they led 2 – 0, but Paul Pogba, playing arguably his best game in a United shirt had other ideas, and, by the end, the City champagne had to be put on ice.

Crossing the divide

The only man to have managed both clubs was *James Mangnall*. He took charge of United between 1903 and 1912, before switching to City until 2024.

The first player to have played for both clubs was Scot *Bob Milarvie* at the end of the 19th century, whilst the most recent was *Owen Hargreaves*.

Other notable names who have pulled on the blue of city and the red of United include *Brian Kidd, Denis Law, Carlos Tevez, Andy Cole and Peter Schmeichel.*

Interesting facts about the rivalry

- The first derby to be played under floodlights was in 1889, and was played in aid of the victims of a local coal mine disaster.
- Steve Coppell played over 300 games for United and his stint as City manager lasted only 32 days.
- Peter Schmeichel was unbeaten in derbies, playing for United between 1991 and 1999, and then City in the 2002 – 2003 season. He never kept a clean sheet once for either side.
- Although they have met in three semi-finals – two in the FA Cup, and once in the League Cup – they have yet to play each other in a major final.

FLA – FLU

FLAMENGO V FLUMINENSE

Location: Rio de Janeiro, Brazil

First Meeting: 7 July 1912

Although Brazil is obsessed with football and it is cited as one of the major reasons for the national team's success over the decades, but it goes much deeper than that. The country has a rich domestic league competition, and, although some of the best talent nowadays is skimmed off early by European clubs, local sides are still supported with passion and intensity.

And arguably, there is no bigger rivalry in Brazil than between the two Rio de Janeiro sides Flamengo and Fluminense (or popularly Fla-Flu). .

The origins of the rivalry

Fluminense were founded in 1902 by Oscar Cox, a sportsman born in Brazil to English parents, and the man often credited with bringing football to the South American country.

The original intention was to call the new team Rio Football Club, but, as there was already a local team with s similar name, they took the Latin name for the Guandu River that flowed thrown the city.

Originally Flamengo were a rowing club, and they only took up football when an internal split in Fluminense in 1911 led to a group of discontented players breaking away. They looked for another club to represent. The very first derby between the two teams took place the following year.

A key development happened in 1936, when Flamengo and Fluminense embraced professionalism, whilst two of Brazil's other big clubs at the time, Vasco de Gama and Botafogo chose to remain amateur.

An influential writer and journalist of the time, Mario Filho had recently acquired the 'Jornal dos Sports" newspaper, and used it as a vehicle to change the sporting culture of the country. He recognised that a newly professionalised sport would need a mass market of fans and also that talking up the derby and the rivalry would boost circulation figures.

One consequence was that a new breed of Brazilian football supporters was born, passionate and committed, rather than mere spectators.

At the same time, there was a social and economic division between the two clubs. Fluminense became a team of the wealthier classes in the city thanks to their English roots. Black or mixed race players were prohibited from representing them. Even today, there is a racist element part of their fan base.

Flamengo chose the opposite path and became a club of the people, with supporters mainly drawn from the working class.

Notable incidents

In 1916, a derby match became one of the first to be suspended in the history of Brazilian football due to a pitch invasion by Fluminense fans who were enraged by the decision of the referee to allow a Flamengo penalty to be re-taken three times.

Arguably the most notorious derby of all was played in November 1941, in a match that became known as "Fla Flu de Lagoa" (The "Fla-Flu" of the Lake). With Fluminense needing just a draw to edge out their rivals for the Rio Championship, they were entertained by Flamengo in a stadium located next to a lake, separated from the Atlantic Ocean by a small strip of land.

Fluminense were leading, but then Flamengo equalised and were pressing for the winner that would give them the title. In desperation, Fluminense, in a bid to waste time, kicked the ball into the lake. A reserve ball was supplied and that too found its way into the lake. When it was retrieved, the Fluminense players promptly declared that the ball had absorbed so much water it was unplayable. And then they kicked it into the lake again!

Eventually the referee blew for full-time and Fluminense had secured the Championship.

Fluminense had a shirt and sponsorship deal with Adidas that expired in 2015. Instead of renewing the deal, the apparel supplier instead negotiated a new ten year deal with Flamengo. A supporters' group, Young Flu, began a campaign to get Adidas off their jerseys and force the club to move to another brand like Nike or Puma, with a campaign known as "#FORAADIDAS".

Most famous matches

Flamengo 4 – 2 Fluminense (December 1991)

The 1991 Carioca Football Championship title was decided over a two legged final. The first leg ended in a 1 – 1 draw, while Flamengo registered a 4 – 2 win in the second leg to lift the title.

Fluminense 3 – 2 Flamengo (June 1995)

This match is best remembered for Flamengo's opener, scored by Renato Gaúcho who deflected a shot into the net with his stomach from a clearly offside position. It became known in Brazil as the "belly game."

Also, passions got the better of the players, as no fewer than four red cards were produced, three of them to Fluminense players. Despite finishing with a two man numerical advantage at the end, Flamengo still lost the game.

Fluminense 3 – 5 Flamengo (January 2010)

Fluminense were leading this match by two goals on the stroke of half-time, but were stunned by Flamengo, as Adriano scored a hat-trick.

Crossing the divide

There have been a number of players who have changed their allegiance over the years. Among the best known are:

Renato Gaúcho

Striker Gaúcho, who played 41 times for Brazil, is a Flamengo legend, having four spells with the club and scoring many a derby goal. But he also had two seasons with Fluminense, scoring against his old side, and he has gone on to manage the two clubs as well.

Gerson

One of the pivotal members of the iconic Brazil World Cup winning team of 1970, Gerson is primarily remembered for his time with Botafogo, but he did play in the Fla-Flu derby for both clubs.

Edinho

Edinho, who was the captain of the 1986 Brazil World Cup team, spent most of his career with Fluminense, although he did have a spell in the colours of their rivals.

Branco

Left-back Branco, who played 72 times for Brazil and featured in two World Cups, began his career with Internacional before joining Fluminense. He would go on to play in Italy and Portugal before returning to Brazil, initially with Grémio, before having a brief stay at Flamengo.

Interesting facts about the rivalry

- The world record attendance for a football match was set in 1963 when 194,603 people saw the clubs play out a scoreless draw. There have been three other attendances which have topped the 150,000 mark.
- It was Mario Filho who coined the term "Fla-Flu" originally.
- One of the first mixed race players in the history of Fluminense, Carlos Alberto, had to cover his face in rice powder before he was allowed to play.
- When Flamengo lose a derby match a popular taunt from Fluminense fans is *"Ela, ela, ela – silencio na favela"* ("Ela, ela, ela – silence in the favela")

EL SÚPER CLÁSICO

CLUB DEPORTIVO GUADALAJARA V CLUB AMERICA

Location: Mexico

First Meeting: 29 July 1943

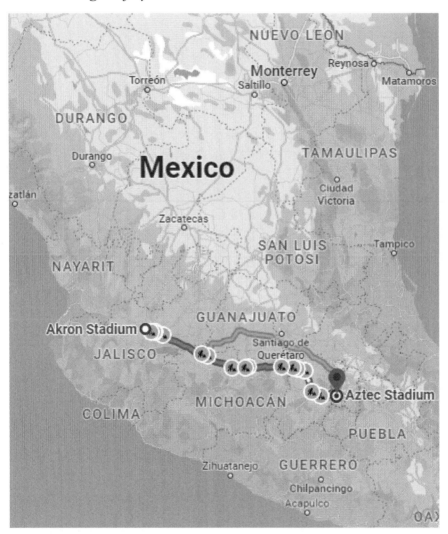

El Súper Clasico describes the traditional rivalry between the two most successful clubs in the history of Mexican football, Club América from Mexico City and Club Deportivo, nicknamed Chivas, from Guadalajara.

Games between the two attract millions of TV viewers, not only in Mexico itself, but also from the large Mexican diaspora community in the USA.

The rivalry also represents historic feelings of regionalism, national pride, economic and social divisions and has been characterised by bad blood between the teams and their supporters.

And the fact that the two teams are often competing against each other for major honours just adds an extra element of spice into what is already a red hot and charged atmosphere.

The origins of the rivalry

Although both teams have longer individual histories, the rivalry dates back to 1943 when Mexican football was reorganised. Three regional leagues joined together to form the Mexican First Division, which is now known as Liga MX. This meant that, having met each other in friendly or cup competitions, games between the two clubs became regular fixtures.

The clubs already had different attitudes and traditions by then. Club América were the first Mexican club team to play outside the country, and supplied the bulk of the players for Mexico's 1928 Olympics and 1930 World Cup squads.

Guadalajara meanwhile had become one of the most popular teams in the country, and one of the most successful, and their policy of only signing Mexican players boosted national pride.

The two clubs have come to represent also the two sides of Mexico's economy. Club América, hailing as they do from the capital Mexico City, are regarded as a team for the rich. For a time they were called "los millionarios" because of the fact that they had spent millions on foreign players in a bid to ensure success.

This followed the purchase of the club by the Azcarraga family, owners of the Televisa media empire, in 1959. They injected massive amounts of funds into Club América; the money was spent on recruiting foreign talent, marketing the team internationally, and opening a brand new state of the art stadium in 1966.

Chivas, on the other hand, position themselves as the "equipo del pueblo" a team for the people, with their policy of signing only Mexican players (although they are well-backed financially as well). Guadalajara claims that it is the most Mexican city because it has produced the three most Mexican things – tequila, mariachi – and Chivas!

Factor in the traditional rivalry between the capital and major provincial cities seen also in many other derbies – France, Spain and Portugal are all instances that come to mind and there is more than reason enough for feelings of resentment, jealously, and enmity.

Notable incidents

During the 1980s several massive brawls marred Clasico games.

The most notable of these occurred in 1983, and is known as "La Bronca del '83), A massive fight was the first time in the history of the fixture that it had been stopped in such a fashion because of violence. All 22 players on the field at the time were suspended by the Mexican Football Association. The match was resumed a month later, with América winning by a single goal.

Fan violence between the two groups of fans is also not uncommon.

In 2012 an exhibition game between the two in Las Vegas saw angry fans rush on to the pitch throwing bottles and cans. It took more than 120 police officers to restore order, and six people required hospital treatment for their injuries. A number of arrests were made.

In 2013 a number of supporters stormed on to the field at the end of a match in Guadalajara, and fans fought in the streets before the match.

Most recently, in March 2022 both sets of fans were asked to wear white for derby matches featuring both the men's and women's teams in protest at the level of violence at all matches in Mexico.

Most famous matches

Club América 5 – 2 Chivas (February 1971)

It is one of the matches that marked the beginning of the rivalry to escalate to new levels. Club América would not only beat their hated rivals in this match, but they would go on to win the league title that season.

Club América 3 – 1 Chivas (June 1984)

The clubs met in the final of the Mexican Cup played over two legs. The first match in Guadalajara ended in a two-all draw, but América won the reverse fixture, with their goalkeeper Miguel Zelada saving a penalty.

Chivas 5 – 0 Club América (August 1996)

It was a day to remember for Chivas fans, but it cost Club América manager Ricardo La Volpe his job.

Club América 2 – 3 Chivas (March 2002)

Chivas won this match by the odd goal in three but the match is best remembered for the performance of referee Gilberto Alcalá who awarded several controversial penalties.

Crossing the divide

Unlike many such rivalries, there has been a constant flow of players between the two clubs over the years, although, because of Chivas' "No non-Mexican' rule, they have all, by necessity, been home grown.

Among the more recent have been:

Ángel Eduardo Reyna Martínez

Attacking midfielder Reyna had played for several local sides before joining Club América in 2009, and it was during his time with them that he broke in to the senior Mexico international squad. He made 103 appearances in three seasons with them, scoring 28 goals, and later joined Chivas but his contract was then terminated by mutual consent after he was accused of a lack of commitment.

Jesús Antonio Molina Granados

Defensive midfielder Jesús Molina, made 126 appearances for Club América between 2011 and 2014, before moving to Santos Laguna and Monterrey, after which he signed for Chivas in 2019, and still plays for them, and is closing in on 100 appearances for the Guadalajara side.

Fernando Rubén González Pineda

Another defensive midfielder, Pineda came through the youth system at Chivas and made his professional debut with them in 2013. He would go on to play for a number of other Mexican clubs including one season at Club América. He completed the full circle and returned to Chivas again.

Alejandro Zendejas Saavedra

Midfielder Zendejas is the most recent to make the switch. He played for Chivas for three seasons between 2016 and 2020 but struggled for first-team football. However, after a spell with Necaxa, he has now joined Club América.

Interesting facts about the rivalry

- Chivas and Club América are the only two clubs never to have been relegated from the top flight of Mexican football.
- A match between the two in 2015 became the most viewed regular season club soccer game in the US in the past five years, attracting a television audience of more than three million.
- Both teams have enjoyed international success. Chivas have won the CONCAF Champions League twice, whilst Club América have won it a record seven times. Along with Egyptian club Al Ahly, they hold the distinction of being the outright record winner of their national league, cup competition and confederation.
- Club América supporters, like Millwall fans, actually revel in the fact that supporters of other teams, especially those from Guadalajara, do not like them, and often wear T-shirts with the slogan "Hate me more."

THE CAIRO DERBY

AL AHLY V ZAMALEK

Location: Cairo, Egypt

First Meeting: 9 February 1917

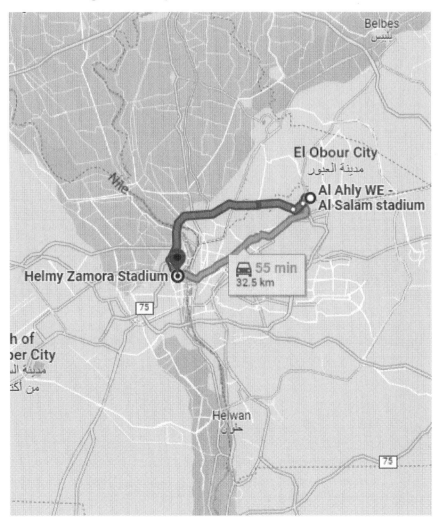

The Cairo derby is a rivalry between the two most successful clubs, not only in the history of Egyptian football, but the whole of Africa as well, Al-Ahly and Zamalek. Matches are fiercely contested, both on and off the field, and are often marred by acts of violence involving both sets of fans and the security forces.

Games between the two are watched not only in Egypt but throughout North Africa and the Middle East. Foreign referees often take charge of the fixture to try and ensure impartiality, whilst all matches are now staged in neutral venues

The origins of the rivalry

The origins can be traced back to when Egypt was under de facto British control between 1882 and 1922. The British army, traders and settlers imported the game of football with them, but it was not until 1907, that Al-Ahly (meaning "The National'), became Egypt's first local club.

They quickly became regarded as a team of the nation, a symbol of resistance, and a rallying cry for the average man to get behind the nationalist cause.

Zamalek were regarded as the team of the foreigners, and the outsiders, and were closely associated with the hated King Farouk (and were even named after him initially) before his abdication.

That gave the derby a political aspect with Zamalek fans regarded as Royalists whilst Al-Ahly supporters were linked with the nationalist cause.

The division were deeper than that. Zamalek is one of the wealthier areas of Cairo, and their team attracted the support of the liberal elite and the intellectuals, whilst Al-Ahly were the team of the poor.

Religion, though, has no part to play in the rivalry. Muslims and Christians are as likely to support one club as the other.

To add to what was already a heady mix of antagonism and mutual antipathy, has been the rise of the ultras, hardcore fans which played a key role in the street protests that brought about the end of the rule of Hosni Mubarak.

These organised fan groups first emerged in 2007, and whilst they became increasingly vocal and anti-authoritarian whilst Mubarak was in power, since his demise, they have begun fighting each other. The result has been a number of deadly riots which have marred Egyptian football in recent years, although the derby has escaped relatively lightly in terms of fan fatalities.

Notable incidents

In 1966 a game between the two was halted when the army stormed the stadium where the match was being played. In the ensuing riot, more than 300 people were injured and an unspecified number of fans lost their lives.

Following a match in the 1971 – 1972 season, the crowd violence between the two sets of fans was so bad that the rest of the Egyptian football league season was called off.

Violence between the two sets of fans is not confined to football. In February 2007 after Al-Ahly narrowly lost a basketball match against their hated rivals, their fans invaded the court, and showered Zamalek players, supporters and management with homemade Molotov cocktails. One Zamalek fan was set alight and badly burned.

Portuguese Manuel Jose, who has managed Al-Ahly three times, was asked to step down from his post for a few weeks when he infuriated religious conservatives in Egypt by stripping off on the touchline during a derby game as a protest against a poor refereeing decision.

Most famous matches

Zamalek 6 – 0 Al-Ahly (Egypt Cup Final) (June 1944)

Zamalek (known at the time as Farouk) equalled their biggest winning margin over their rivals, having previously won by the same score-line in a league fixture back in 1942.

Al Ahly 3 – 2 Zamalek (August 1985)

An internal conflict between Al-Ahly club president and manager saw the president decide to pull all of his first-team from this fixture in 1985. Instead, they fielded a side made up exclusively of youth team players, who still went on to win.

Zamalek 3 – 1 Al Ahly (August 2016)

In August 2016, the two sides met in the final of the Egypt Cup and it resulted in a win for Zamalek, who raced into an early two goal lead, before Al-Ahly pulled a goal back before half-time. A third goal eleven minutes after the break put the result beyond doubt.

Al-Ahly 2 – 1 Zamalek (November 2020)

In 2020, the pair met in the final of the CAF Champions League, the first time they had played each other in the final of an international competition. Al-Ahly won the match 2 - 1, sealing a record ninth win in the competition.

Crossing the divide

Although there are players who have appeared for both clubs, given the history between the two sides, their numbers are relatively less. Here are some of the names.

Hussein Hegazi

Hegazi was the first to make the switch, something the forward was to do several times in his career. He played for Al-Ahly between 1915 and 1923 before moving across the city. After five years at Zamalek he returned to play another season with Al-Ahly. He rounded off his playing career back at Zamalek.

Ibrahim Hassan

Hassan, who played over 200 times for the Egyptian national side, was an Ah-Ahly stalwart for the best part of 15 years. But he was to end his career wearing Zamalek colours.

Moamen Zakaria

Zakaria made his name at Zamalek where the winger scored nine goals in 35 appearances before transferring to Al-Ahly. His career was cut short when he was diagnosed with Motor Neuron Disease in 2020.

Interesting facts about the rivalry

- There have been a number of withdrawals from derby fixtures over the years. In 1975, the Zamalek side walked off the pitch after the referee missed a clear offside, and they staged a similar protest in

1989-1990 season in protest after the French referee ruled out a goal for them. Ah Ahly refused to play against their rivals in the first round of the Egyptian League Cup in 2001, and, three years later, withdrew from the Arab Champions League because the Arab Football Union refused to allow them to add new players to their roster.

- In February 2020, the arrival of the Zamalek team bus was delayed due to traffic congestion caused by heavy rain in the Cairo area. Al-Ahly were awarded a 2 – 0 victory.

- In a bid to discourage opposing fans from attending the match, Zamalek raised ticket prices before the first game of the 2006 – 2007 season to unprecedented level. The plan backfired on both fronts. Not only was the crowd dramatically down on the normal attendance, but Al-Ahly won 2 – 1.

- The two have met nine times in the CAF Champions League and Zamalek have yet to win a game. Al-Ahly have won six matches and the other three have been drawn.

TYNE WEAR DERBY

NEWCASTLE UNITED V SUNDERLAND

Location: Tyne and Wear, Northwest England

First Meeting: 1883

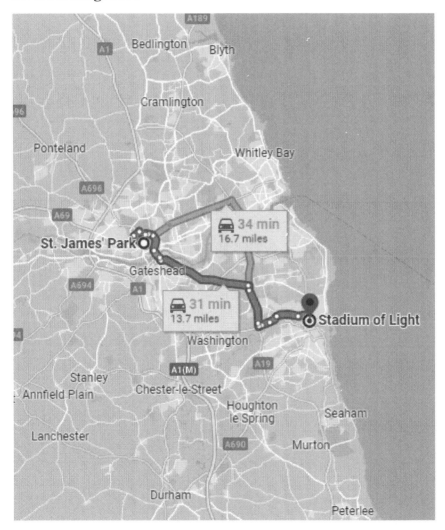

Whilst Sunderland's current exile from top flight football may have brought a temporary cessation of hostilities on the pitch, the Tyne Wear derby remains one of the most fiercely contested in England, with two of the most passionate fan bases.

With roots which can be traced back hundreds of years to long standing antagonisms between the two cities of Newcastle and Sunderland, it is a fixture that continues to stir the blood and the emotions, and it has seen more than its fair share of violence between supporters over the years.

If there is one thing fans of both clubs can agree on, though, it is that, on derby day, winning is everything.

The origins of the rivalry

The origins of the rivalry between the two football clubs can be traced back to a longer standing rivalry between the cities of Newcastle and Sunderland, which are 12 miles apart in North-East England. During the English civil war in the 17th century, rich merchants in Newcastle held financial advantages and privileges over their counterparts in Sunderland, which led to the latter becoming a parliamentary stronghold.

And then in the 17th and 18th century, the two cities found themselves on opposite sides again, this time during the Jacobite risings. Newcastle supported the ruling Hanoverians, whilst Sunderland backed the Scottish Stuarts.

In more recent times, Sunderland's enmity towards Newcastle was further stoked by the inclusion of the city into the newly created Tyne and Wear County in 1974, following a local government reorganisation.

This unpopular move saw Sunderland leave County Durham and instead join with their neighbours in the newly created county, where they allegedly have been made to feel like second class citizens ever since. For instance, when the Tyne & Wear Metro public transport system was opened in 1980, it did not initially serve the people of Wearside, even though they felt that they had paid their fair share towards it over the years in the form of local taxes. It would not be until 2002 that an extension was built linking the system to Sunderland.

The current day rivalry does have its comic side. For example, some Newcastle fans report to eat bacon because of its red and white colouring.

And there are some Sunderland supporters who, even to this day, will not eat the popular breakfast cereal Sugar Puffs because it was once advertised by former Newcastle United manager Kevin Keegan.

Notable incidents

The fixture has been synonymous with violence and football hooliganism over the years. In 1980 with the pair meeting in a play-off semi-final and Sunderland winning 2 – 0, Newcastle fans invaded the pitch in the hope of getting the game called off. More than 160 arrests were made by the police.

What was described as one of the worst instances of football fighting ever witnessed in the UK occurred in March 2002, when Seaburn Casuals, who were affiliated with Sunderland clashed with the Newcastle Gremlins. The pre-arranged fixture near the North Shields Ferry Terminal saw the leaders of both sets of fans jailed for four years, whilst another 28 were jailed for various offences.

The following year 95 fans were arrested after fans of both club clashed in Sunderland city centre before an England qualifying match against Turkey was played in the city.

Headlines were made all over the world in April 2013 when some Newcastle fans rioted on the streets of the city following a home defeat by Sunderland. One irate fan punched a police horse called Bud, and earned a year in jail for his troubles.

Most famous matches

Newcastle 1 – 9 Sunderland (December 1908)

This remains the biggest ever win in the history of the fixture, and is remarkable because the scores were level at half-time. But after the break the Black Cats found the net eight times in a 28 minute spell.

Newcastle 3 – 1 Sunderland (January 1985)

Newcastle welcomed 1985 in style with this New Year's Day win over their rivals. Peter Beardsley scored a hat-trick, including a penalty, following the award of which former Magpies player Howard Gayle was sent off for his protests to the referee.

Newcastle 1 – 2 Sunderland (August 1999)

Newcastle manager Ruud Gullit at the time went into this match desperately needing a win to hang on to his job. Beforehand he controversially dropped his twin strikers, Alan Shearer and Duncan Ferguson, and when his side went ahead the move seemed to have paid off. But as the rain poured down in the second-half, Sunderland came from behind to win. Gullit was sacked three days later.

Sunderland 1 – 4 Newcastle (April 2006)

Sunderland led for much of the game, but then Newcastle stormed back with four goals, among them a penalty from club legend Alan Shearer. It was his final Premier League goal.

Crossing the divide

Surprisingly the two clubs have shared a number of personnel in common over the years.

Two men have managed both clubs, *Sam Allardyce* and *Steve Bruce*, whilst *Bob Stokoe*, who managed Sunderland to their shock FA Cup Final win over Leeds United in 1973, had also won the cup in his playing days with Newcastle.

Among the most famous players to wear both colours are:

Len Shackleton

The man known as "The Crown Prince of Soccer" scored six goals on his Newcastle debut, but, two years later, he fell out with the club's directors, and was sold to Sunderland for a then British record fee. He would go on to make 348 appearances for the Wearside club, scoring 100 goals.

Chris Waddle

Waddle joined Newcastle from non-league football, having had an unsuccessful trial with Sunderland. The winger would make a name for himself on Tyneside before moving to Tottenham and then Marseille and Sheffield Wednesday and forging a successful England career. He also played seven games for Sunderland in 1997.

Andy Cole

Cole began his career at Arsenal but it was when he joined Newcastle he made a name for himself, scoring 68 goals in 84 appearances. That earned him a high profile move to Manchester United, but he returned to the North-East at the tail-end of his career for a brief spell with Sunderland.

Shay Given

Goalkeeper Given began his professional career with Blackburn, where he enjoyed several loan spells, one of them to Sunderland. Newcastle signed him permanently in 1997, and he would go on to make 462 appearances for them. He later had spells with Manchester City, and Aston Villa.

Interesting facts about the rivalry

- Only the Merseyside derby between Liverpool and Everton has seen more bookings in the Premier League era, despite the fact that Sunderland have not been in the top flight since the end of the 2016 – 2017 season.
- The current head to head record is exactly even. They have faced each other 156 times and both have won 53 times, whilst the other matches have ended in draws.
- Both clubs are nicknamed after wildlife. New castle are called "The Magpies" after the colour of their shirts. The name "The Black Cats" for Sunderland, according to myth dates back to 1805 when Joshua Dunn, a local volunteer in a militia unit, fled from the howling of a black cat one night. His battery guarding the River Wear became known as "The Black Cats."

THE KOLKATA DERBY

MOHUN BAGAN V EAST BENGAL

Location: Kolkata, West Bengal

First Meeting: 8 August 1921

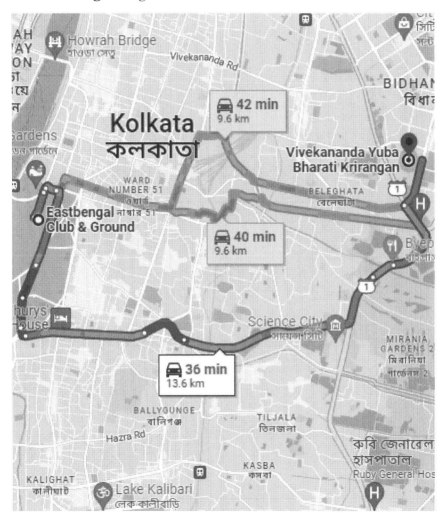

The Kolkata Derby between Mohun Bagan and East Bengal is the oldest football rivalry in Asia, dating back more than a hundred years. It is not just a sporting rivalry either, but one that has its roots in the culture and history of India's Bengali population.

And whilst foreigners may believe that cricket is king in India and that support for other sports is minimal, anybody who is in Kolkata on derby day may choose to differ.

With both clubs now part of the Indian Super League (ISL), matches between the two are likely to grow in prominence.

The origins of the rivalry

Bengalis are people from the eastern part of India. Those from the eastern region (now Bangladesh) are called "Bangals", whilst those from the western region are called "Ghotis"

Although ostensibly part of the Bengali community, there are several differences between the Ghotis and Bangals in terms of dialect, economic backgrounds, dressing sense, and cuisine.

Mohun Bagan was established in 1889, and whilst their players were a mix of both communities, they were predominantly run by Ghotis. Originally known as The Mariners, they were the first all Indian club to beat a British team to win a major domestic trophy.

Ghotis were more financially affluent than the Bangals, who were mainly immigrants or refugees.

East Bengal owe their existence to a match that was due to be played in 1920 between Mohun Bagan and another Kolkata club, Jorabagan.

When Jorabagan chose not to field their star player, Sailesh Bose, Suresh Chandra Chaudhuri, who was their vice president and leading industrialist, was perplexed and demanded to know the reasons why the player had not been selected. His arguments for Bose's inclusion fell on deaf ears, with other club officials implying it was because he was from East Bengal.

Incensed, Chaudhuri stormed off, taking Bose and a few others with him and, within a week, he had established East Bengal, their objective being to represent the immigrant population in Kolkata.

Between 1921 and 1924 the two teams faced each other several times, although it was not until 1925 the first official Kolkata Derby was staged (East Bengal won the match by a single goal).

In 1947, the partition of India saw a mass exodus of Bangals from Bangladesh to West Bengal, further strengthening the East Bengal fan base.

The derby has also become synonymous with what have become known as the 'Fish Wars". Bengalis love their fish, although they have different preferences – Bangals are known for their appreciation of hilsa, whilst Ghotis' choice is prawn.

On derby days, the price of both these sea food tends to soar due to high demand, and that of the winning team can reach astronomical levels in the days afterwards.

It was not uncommon for neighbourhoods in Kolkata to be painted in team colours before a derby. Mohun Bagan's green and maroon stripes are meant to represent affluence and legacy, whilst their logo, a bat with its sails up, symbolises progress with the passing of time.

East Bengal, meanwhile wear red and gold shirts with a logo of a flaming torch, designed to indicate the desire and fire among refugees to succeed, whatever the odds.

Noticeable Incidents

The darkest day in the history of the rivalry came on 16th August 1980 at Eden Gardens in Kolkata, when 16 fans died, and hundreds more were injured. Trouble began in the second half of the match, when the referee showed two red cards, one to Dilip Patil of East Bengal, and the other to Bidesh Basu of Mohun Bagan.

This created an uproar among the fans, who, although normally are segregated, were sitting together on that occasion. Eventually, it resulted in a stampede, which led to the loss of life and the other casualties.

An iconic figure during derby matches is the street seller known as Lozenge Masi (Candy Aunt) who makes a living selling hard candy during East

Bengal matches. Jamuna Das, an avid East Bengal fan, can also be found leading the chanting of her team's fans, dressed head to toe in East Bengal colours.

Famous Matches

The 1997 Federation Cup semi-final between the two sides was attended by over 130,000 fans at the Salt Lake Stadium in Kolkata, with many thousands more outside unable to get into the ground. It remains the most attended sporting event in Indian history. Baichung Bhatia scored a hat-trick in East Bengal colours, elevating him to an instant hero status, as his side won 4 - 1.

The 100th derby was played in 1967 in the Rovers Cup final, East Bengal emerging the winners with a two goal victory.

The bicentenary derby in April 1993 in the Airlines Cup final was won by Mohun Bagan 6 – 5 after extra time.

The tricentenary derby in January 2012 in the Calcutta Football League was won by Mohun Bagan 2 – 0.

On 27th November 2020, the two sides met for the first time in the ISL, ATK Mohun Bagan winning 2 – 0.

Crossing the divide

Goutam Sarkar, Prasantha Banerjee, Dulal Biswas and *Renedy Singh* have the distinction of having captained both sides.

Baichung Bhatia is the top scorer in derby fixtures. For East Bengal he scored 13 goals, before switching to Mohun Bagan where he managed six more.

Interesting facts about the rivalry

- The record for the fastest goal in derby history belongs to Md. Akbar of Mohun Bagan. Just 16 seconds of the 1976 match had elapsed when he scored from a header. It proved to be the only goal of the game.
- In January 2020, Mohun Bagan merged with another Kolkata club, ATK (Atlético de Kolkata) to become ATK Mohun Bagan. The

merger was designed, in part, to allow Mohun Bagan to enter the ISL. The new team retained the green and maroon colours.

- After his team were beaten 5 – 0 at home in 1975, Umakanto Palodhi, a Mohun Bagan supporter, took his own life. In his suicide note he penned the lines *"in my next birth, I will take revenge by becoming a Mohun Bagan player"*.
- That defeat might have been even worse, had Shyam Thapa not missed a penalty for East Bengal.

THE PAULISTA DERBY

CORINTHIANS V PALMEIRAS

Location: Sao Paulo, Brazil

First Meeting: 6 May 1917

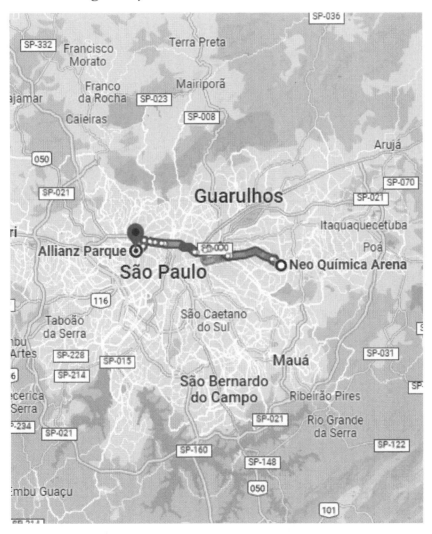

In a country that is generally football mad, nowhere is it taken more seriously than in Brazil's São Paulo, a vast sprawling metropolis home to more than 12 million people.

There are actually three major clubs in São Paulo – Corinthians, São Paulo F.C, and Palmeiras, whilst Santos from the nearby beach city, are part of the mix as well, and each have their own animosities and grievances against the others.

However, the biggest mutual rivalry is the Paulista derby between Corinthians and Palmeiras, despite the fact that they share similar backgrounds.

The origins of the rivalry

Both teams were formed by groups of factory workers in the 1910s.

After the English amateur club Corinthian FC made a tour of the southeast of Brazil, thrashing all comers in terms of local opposition, a group of five workers, who also happened to be friends, got together in the central neighbourhood of Bom Retiro, and decided to form their own club. They called it Sporting Club Corinthians Paulista (honouring the English club in their name).

Four years later, Palmeiras were formed in similar circumstances. After seeing Italian clubs Pro Vercelli and Torino play in the city, immigrant Italian factory workers also were inspired to create their own club. Initially called Palestra Italia, it was renamed Palmeiras during World War 2, after the Brazilian government decreed that football organisations were forbidden from using names related to Axis powers..

Both teams from the outset had a distinctly working class following. The difference was that whilst Corinthians modelled themselves as the "team of the people" Palmeiras positioned themselves as the club of the city's large Italian community.

Many of the old distinctions between the teams and their supporter bases have become blurred over the years. It is now not uncommon to find whole neighbourhoods and even families split in their support. And there is one area in which they find common cause.

Both the sets of supporters hate São Paulo F.C

Notable incidents

In 1993, there was a mass brawl involving fans of both clubs, plus São Paulo F.C in the centre of the city. The clubs' main supporter groups run samba schools which compete in the annual Carnival, among them are Gavioes da Fiel (Faithful Hawks) of Corinthians and the Mancha Verde (The Green Phantom Blot) of Palmeiras. Whilst the exact origins of what happened are disputed, the outcome was two dead and scores injured.

In 2016, when shots were exchanged between warring supporter groups, an innocent bystander was struck and killed by a stray bullet.

In 2017, a Palmeiras fan died of stab wounds after a clash with Corinthians supporters.

In January 2021 a Corinthian fan died after clashes between rival groups of fans. They attacked each other with sticks and stones, but the situation escalated when a Palmeiras fan produced a firearm. 21 Palmeiars fans were arrested,.

Most famous matches

Corinthians 8 – 0 Palmeiras (November 1933)

The score-line remains the biggest margin in the history of the fixture, but much of what happened on the day is lost to history, apart from the fact that Luis Imparato scored a hat-trick and provided two assists, whilst his strike partner Romeu Pelliciari netted four times.

Corinthians 2 – 0 Palmeiras (2 – 4 pens) (May 1999)

Palmeiras won their one and only Copa Libertadores in 1999, and it was particularly satisfying that they knocked out their great rivals at the quarter-final stage on their own ground. Palmeiras won the first leg 2 – 0, but when the score-line was the same after extra time in the reverse fixture, it went to penalties. Two saves from goalkeeper Marcos would prove to be the difference.

Palmeiras 3 – 2 Corinthians (5 - 4 pens) (June 2000)

The pair met in the semi-finals of the Copa Libertadores, with a final spot against Boca Juniors up for grabs. Palmeiras, the defending champions had lost a dramatic first leg 4 – 3, but fought back to win the second leg and it needed penalties to decide the winner.

Palmeiras goalkeeper Marcos made himself the hero on the night by saving Marcelinhos's spot kick.

Corinthians 0 – 0 Palmeiras (December 2011)

Although this may not have had any goals, there was a lot riding on this match, with the home side needing just a draw to clinch the league title. They managed it, but not before the referee brandished four red cards as Palmeiras tried to upset the party.

Crossing the divide

There have been some who have dared to make what is still regarded by some fans as a treacherous move.

Among the best known are:

Rivaldo

Although Rivaldo is best remembered for winning the Ballon d'Or with Barcelona and the World Cup with Brazil in 2002, earlier in his career he had spent two seasons on loan with Corinthians, before joining Palmeiras.

Vagner Love

The much travelled striker began his career with Palmeiras, and then returned to them on loan when he was with CSKA Moscow. After a spell in the Chinese Super League he returned to Brazil, this time with Corinthians. Four years later he returned for a second season.

Interesting facts about the rivalry

- In 1918, before an early match between the two clubs, the players of Palmeiras passed by a pension where those from Corinthians happened to be having lunch. One of the Palmeiras players took an ox bone, wrote on it 'Corinthians is chicken soup for Palestra''. Palmeiras were winning the subsequent game, but Corinthians fought back to draw and they have kept the ox bone in their trophy room ever since.

- In 1945, the pair played a match designed to raise funds for the Brazilian Communist Party (PCB).
- There have been four attendances in excess of 100,000 in the history of the fixture, with the biggest crowd being the 120,522 fans who saw Palmeiras win 1 – 0 at the Morumbi Stadium in December 1974.
- The longest undefeated run in the fixture is twelve games set by Palmeiras between May 1930 and August 1934, and again between February 2006 and February 2010.

EL DERBI MADRILEÑO

REAL MADRID V ATLETICO DE MADRID

Location: Madrid, Spain

First Meeting: 2 December 1906

Although El Clásico is now considered the biggest rivalry in Spain, that was not always the case, and, with the cities of Madrid and Barcelona lying some 400 miles apart, it is not a derby anyway in the strict sense of the word.

Indeed, legendary Real player Alfredo di Stéfano once said 'forget Barcelona …the team that can frustrate us is Atlético".

It is a rivalry reaching back over 100 years, and reflects, in part, the history of Spain itself in the intervening period.

The origins of the rivalry

The rivalry between the two clubs began in the early years of the 20th century.

The rivalry between the two clubs began in the early years of the 20th century.

Madrid Football Club were founded in 1902, and through a series of mergers and acquisitions absorbed many of the smaller teams in the Madrid area, and also signed many of the best players from clubs who were not involved in this acquisition process. The club became known as Real (Royal), a title bestowed by the King of Spain on his favourite teams.

The exception to this rule was Athletic Club Madrid. They actually began life as a subsidiary of Athletic Bilbao after a group of young Basque students were given remission to set up a team in the Madrid area (even today the two teams share the same red and white striped kit).

They managed to keep hold of their best players, and many supporters of the original clubs that had been absorbed by Real switched their allegiance to Atlético.

During the Spanish Civil War and the period immediately after it, Atlético became associated with the military air force, and for a while became the most successful club in Spain. However, the preference of the Franco regime then shifted to Real, as they sought to make political capital from their success on the European stage.

Atlético fans would chant that Real were "*El equipo del gobierno, la vergüenza del país*" – "The team of the government, the shame of the country", although that does not necessarily mean they were left-leaning with Rayo Vallecano having better claims to be the real "leftish" club in the region.

Nowadays, whether somebody supports Real or Atlético is mainly due to identity, and people tend to follow the team that their father supported, and their father before him.

There is also a geographical split. Atlético are more popular in the south of the city, which is where their stadium is located. Real, on the other hand, are based in the north, generally a more affluent area, and that is where most of their support is based (although they, more than their rivals, have a worldwide fan base).

Notable incidents

Whilst nowadays both clubs sign players from anywhere, irrespective of creed, it was not always the case. For a time, Real adopted a racist attitude, with president Santiago Bernabéu explaining the club's refusal to sign Portuguese star Eusebio at the end of the 1960s as *Mientras yo viva, aquí no jugará ningún negro ni un blanco con bigote* ("As Long as I live, no black or white with a moustache, will play here")

And in 1970s, Real fans mockingly used to call Atlético "Los Indios" (Indians) because of the number of players from Latin America that they had.

Although the rivalry is fierce and intense, there is seldom the violence and hooliganism as seen in other such fixtures. For example, when the two sides met in the Champions League final in Lisbon in 2014, fans shared cars and transport together and there was no trouble before or after the game.

When the two met in a post season exhibition match in 2019 in the USA, it was the first time, apart from the Champions League finals, that the pair had played a derby outside Spain. It also was a record score-line, Atlético winning 7 – 3.

Most famous matches

Real Madrid 1 – 3 Atlético Madrid (1960 Copa del Generalísimo final) (June 1960)

This was the Real side which won five successive European Cups, but Atlético were going through a golden period themselves and won the Spanish Cup at the home of their great rivals.

Real Madrid 2 – 2 Atlético (January 2003)

It was a typically bad tempered affair. Luis Figo had scored two but missed from the penalty spot for what would have been his hat-trick. Atlético gained a controversial late equaliser and, as tempers flared, Real defender Ivan Helguera and Atlético's Garcia Calvo both saw red.

Real Madrid 4 – 1 Atlético (Champions League Final 2014) (May 2014)

The two clubs met in the final of the Champions League in Lisbon, and, for long periods, Atlético seemed on the verge of winning the trophy for the first time, after scoring in the first half. But deep into injury time Sergio Ramos scored, and then goals from Gareth Bale, Marcelo and Cristiano Ronaldo won it for Real in extra time.

Real Madrid 1 – 1 Atlético (pen 5 – 3) (Champions League Final 2016) (May 2016)

It was a case of Deja-vu two years later in Milan. This time Ramos opened the scoring, but Yannick Carrasco equalised, and with no further goals after extra time, it went to a penalty shoot-out. Real converted all theirs, but Juanfran missed from 12 yards.

Crossing the divide

There have been a number of players who have appeared for both City rivals, including *Pérez Paya*, who won the league with Atlético in the 1950 – 1951 season, before winning more La Liga titles with Real.

More recently, current Real keeper *Thibaut Courtois* emulated the feat. He won La Liga in 2013 – 2014 with Atlético, and then, after returning to Spain after his spell in England with Chelsea, has won two more titles with Real.

Among others to make the journey are:

Santiago Bernabéu

Real's president for 35 years, who is regarded as one of the most important figures in the history of the club, played for both clubs in his brief playing career.

Hugo Sánchez

Regarded as one of the finest Mexican players ever, Sánchez joined Atlético in 1981, and, in four seasons with them, scored 82 goals in 152 appearances. He then joined Real where he was to have even greater success, scoring 208 goals, and winning five league titles.

Bernd Schuster

German international midfielder Schuster is one of an elite group of men to have played for all the biggest clubs in Spain. He first joined Barcelona, before moving on to Real, and then Atlético, winning league titles with the first two, and the Copa del Rey with all three.

Alvaro Morata

Morata is still on the books of Atlético, although he has spent the last two seasons on loan at Juventus. His spent his youth career at both clubs, as well as Getafe, making his Real debut in 2010.

He signed for Juventus before returning to Real and then was sold to Chelsea, but having failed to settle in England, he was loaned to Atlético, before joining them permanently.

Interesting facts about the rivalry

- There are two famous fountains in the centre of Madrid, which are considered symbols of the two teams. When Real win, their fans head to the fountain of Cybele, the Roma goddess of fertility and agriculture. When Atlético win, their supporters head to the fountain of Neptune, the Roma god of sea and freshwater.
- Another tradition is that league championships are celebrated at the city's Harvest Golden Square. Although it has become synonymous with Real fans in recent years, the ritual was started by Atlético fans in 1977 when they won La Liga.
- Between 2000 and 2013, Atlético did not manage a single win in the fixture. The best they achieved was the occasional draw.
- Atlético have won the Copa del Rey 10 times, and nine of those victories have come in Real's own stadium, the Bernabéu. The exception was their 1995 victory over Barcelona which took place in Zaragoza.

THE SEVILLE DERBY

REAL BETIS V SEVILLA

Location: Seville, Spain

First Meeting: 8 October 1915

Although international headlines tend to be made by the El Clasico clashes between Barcelona and Real Madrid, Spain is actually home to many local rivalries, and none is more fiercely contested than El Gran Derbi, featuring the two main teams based in Seville, Sevilla and Real Betis (originally Real Betis Balompié).

Whilst Seville as a city may be better known to outsiders for its architecture, flamenco dancing, and also for its intense summer heat, this is a football crazy city, and any visitor will immediately notice red and white, or green and white colours displayed in a shop or apartment window, or reference to one of the clubs in graffiti, or stuck to a pole.

And come derby day, when police throng the streets in a bid to try and keep rival fans apart, there can be no doubt as to what is at stake.

The origins of the rivalry

Sevilla were the first to be formed in 1890 by a mix of both locals and English and Scottish immigrants. Fifteen years later they played a match against Recreativo Huelva which was the first ever sanctioned game of football in Spain.

From the outset Sevilla gained the reputation of being an international club, and they attracted fans from all across the capital, in particular from middle-class districts.

Betis owe their origins to a dispute with Sevilla. In 1907, Sevilla allegedly refused to sign a player from the working class Triana neighbourhood of the city. Some members of the club were enraged, feeling that this smacked of elitism, and that active discrimination was being practiced against those who hailed from certain localities.

There was a walk-out and Real Betis Balompié were formed in protest.

The club was formed with the specific intent of being the "people's club" not only of Sevilla but of the surrounding Andalucía region. They chose to play in green and white because those are the dominant colours on the Andalucian flag. Betis is the Roman word for the river that runs through Seville, whilst Balompié (since dropped) is an old Spanish term for football.

By adding Real" (Royal) to the name, they became one of King's chosen team in football, thus cementing their status as the team of Spain in the city.

Despite this, there is no agreement between fans as to who is the real "people's club" of Seville, and both claim the title for themselves. There are no specific districts reserved exclusively for Betis or Seville fans; they are scattered all over the city, and likely to live next door to each other.

There are plenty of working class Sevilla supporters, whilst the Betis stadium is located in one of the more up market areas of the city.

Sevilla are undoubtedly top dogs when it comes to achievements on the pitch. Not only have they won a La Liga title, five Spanish Cups, and a Spanish Super Cup, but they have also enjoyed unparalleled success in the Europa League, winning it in three consecutive years between 2014 and 2016.

By comparison, Betis have only won the league once, and their Spanish Cup win in 2022 was their first trophy of any kind in 17 years.

Despite this support for them remains undiminished among their passionate fan base.

Notable incidents

Back in 1918, Sevilla player Manuel Perez was stabbed in the buttocks by a Betis fan.

In 1978, Betis were relegated, despite finishing above Elche and Cadiz, and level on points with both Hercules and Espanyol, but with a much better goal difference. However, they still went down because of the system in use in Spain at the time which compared home defeats with away wins.

However, allegations surrounded the role of Sevilla in their fate, because comfortably in mid-table, they supposedly threw the game against Alicante just to get their rivals relegated.

During a match in 2002, Betis goalkeeper Toni Prats was attacked by a Sevilla supporter who jumped on his back wielding a lighter before security forces were able to intervene and have him arrested.

In 2007, Sevilla coach Juande Ramos was knocked unconscious after he was struck by a bottle thrown by a Betis fan. He was in the technical area during a Copa del Rey quarter-final between the two clubs, and as his team celebrated scoring a goal the bottle was thrown. Despite the fact he was knocked unconscious, some Betis fans believed that he had faked the whole event. The incident is known as the "botellazo" in Spain.

In January 2018, 24 fans, all young males, were arrested on the eve of the derby after a mass brawl broke out on one of the bridges leading into the city.

In January 2022, the Copa del Rey tie was suspended after Sevilla midfielder Joan Jordan was struck on the head by a projectile thrown from the crowd, shortly after Betis had scored an equaliser.

The match was completed several weeks later behind closed doors.

Most famous matches

Betis 3 – 3 Sevilla (April 2013)

Sevilla seemed to have the points wrapped up as they went three goals to the good after just half an hour, before Betis pulled two goals back. A touchline incident which provoked a mass brawl saw the visitors reduced to ten men, but they looked like holding on for the win, until a late equaliser.

Sevilla 3 – 5 Betis (January 2018)

One of the highest scoring games in recent Spanish history began with a Betis goal after just 30 seconds. The scores were level at half time, and then the visitors went two goals up. Sevilla got one back and was pressing for the equaliser, when Betis scored again on the break, deep into injury time.

Sevilla 3 – 2 Betis (April 2019)

Not only was this a match of high drama but it was a game of beautiful goals as well, both teams trying to out-do the other when it came to artistry. Most neutrals agreed it was the best game seen in Spain that year.

Crossing the divide

There have actually been comparatively few players who have appeared for both clubs, and only nine have played in Seville derbies for both teams.

Joaquin Jiménez Postigo

Defender Postigo has the distinction of being the only man to have La Liga titles with both clubs (Betis won their only league title in the 1934-35 season).

Diego Rodriguez

Another defender, Rodriguez made the switch in 1988.

Luis Aragones

The man who coached Spain to success in the Euros in 2008, spent three seasons as a player with Betis, and later managed both clubs in derby matches.

Interesting facts about the rivalry

- The first derby was reportedly played on Valentine's Day in 1909 but the result of that has been lost to history. The first recorded match took place in 1915, and, after Sevilla won it by a single goal, they paraded a trophy around the pitch.
- Sevilla once won the derby 22 – 0. In 1918, when two of their star players were banned by decree from taking part because they were still completing military service, Betis sent a team of children to represent them.
- They are only two of the nine clubs ever to win the La Liga title. Betis were the first to achieve the feat in 1934/1935 under Irish manager Patrick O'Connell, and Sevilla emulated them a decade later.
- They have met once in European competition in the round of 16 of the Europa League in the 2013/2014 season. Sevilla won the two legged tie on penalties and went on lift the trophy that year.

DER KLASSIKER

FC BAYERN MUNICH V BORUSSIA DORTMUND

Location: Germany

First Meeting: 16 October 1965

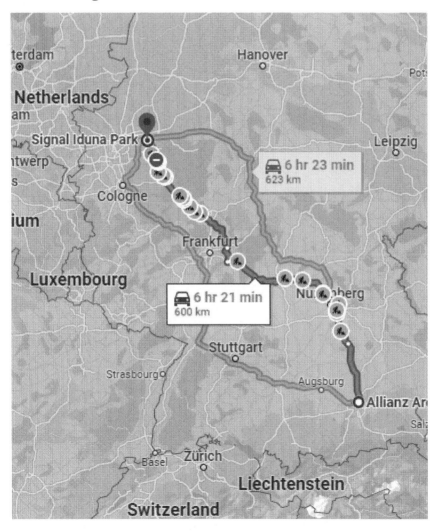

Unlike many derbies, the rivalry between Borussia Dortmund and Bayern Munich is no neighbourhood turf war. The two cities are almost 600 kilometres apart, and there is no particular animosity that can be traced to economic, social, religious or political differences.

Indeed, before the formation of the Bundesliga in 1963, the two teams rarely played each other because German football was organised on a regional basis and the two were in different leagues.

And, whilst Bayern were winning three successive cups in the 1970s, Dortmund spent four consecutive seasons languishing in the second division.

It means that the history of their rivalry is more recent and can be traced back to the emergence of Dortmund as the most consistent challenger to Bayern's dominance in German football.

The origins of the rivalry

As stated above, the rivalry between the two clubs is different. There are no political, social, economic or religious factors behind it, nor can the close proximity be blamed.

In this case it is purely sporting, and can be attributed to the rise of Dortmund to become the most consistent challenger to Bayern's dominance in Germany. The Bavarian club have still won the last ten Bundesliga titles, but should they slip, Dortmund are the most likely to take advantage.

And Der Klassiker has now become of national importance. Dortmund have acquired the status of many people's second favourite club (apart from Schalke fans, of course).

Those fed up with Bayern winning everything like nothing better to get behind a team that can give them a good game.

Notable incidents

At the start of the 1986/87 season, the teams drew 2 -2. However, the match will always be remembered for the legendary miss by Dortmund's Frank Mill. The forward had already beaten Bayern goalkeeper Jean-Marie Pfaff, but, with the goal gaping, hit the post instead. It remains one of the worst misses seen in German football.

During a game in 1997, Bayern captain Lothar Matthaus made a gesture following a challenge by Andreas Möller, rubbing his eyes as if crying, making out that Möller, who was a friend of his off the pitch, was a bit soft. It became known in Germany as the "cry baby" incident.

In 1999 Bayern goalkeeper Oliver Khan earned himself the nickname "Kung-Fu-Kahn" when he jumped towards the approaching Stephane Chapuisat with his leg outstretched. As there was no contact and the offside flag had already been raised, the referee took no action, and Kahn later saved a penalty as Bayern came from two down to salvage a point.

A top of the table clash in 2002 saw Bayern beaten by Dortmund, the defending champions. However, the hero of the day for Dortmund was towering forward Jan Koller. He scored for his side in the eighth minute, but, after Jens Lehmann was sent off, the Czech was forced to go in goal for much of the second half because Dortmund had used all their substitutes. So well did he perform, that he was named by Kicker as the "Goalkeeper of the week"

Most famous matches

Bayern 11 - 1 Dortmund (November 1971)

The biggest score-line of the history of the fixture saw Bayern run riot with Gerd Müller scoring four, and Uli Hoeness a brace.

Dortmund 1 – 1 Bayern (April 2001)

This was a top of the table clash, with Dortmund trailing Bayern by a single point going into the game. It developed into a highly fraught affair which saw referee Hartmut Strampe dish out eleven yellow and two red cards, the most ever in a single Bundesliga game. The point was good enough to keep Bayern ahead in the standings, and they went on to secure the league title.

Dortmund 1 – 0 Bayern (April 2012)

It is the match that transformed Der Klassiker into a global affair for many fans. Dortmund, under Jurgen Klopp, playing his brand of "heavy metal" football won thanks to a late goal from Robert Lewandowski. Arjen Robben missed a late penalty and Dortmund went on to win the title.

Bayern 2 – 1 Dortmund (Champions League final) (May 2013)

In 2013, the German giants met in the final of the Champions League at Wembley in London. Mario Mandzukić gave Bayern the lead, only for Ilkay Gündogan to equalise from the penalty spot soon afterwards. Arjen Robben scored the winner in extra time.

Crossing the divide

In recent years, it has been by no means unusual for some big names to move between the two clubs, especially from Dortmund to Bayern, the biggest club in Germany, where they can expect to be paid better and regularly contend for silverware. However, moves do happen the other way as well.

Here are four examples:

Robert Lewandowski

Lewandowski may just have signed for Barcelona but he leaves Bayern as a club legend having scored 344 goals in 375 games for them. He joined them from Dortmund having scored 103 goals in 187 games in Yellow and Black colours.

Mats Hummels

Centre-back Hummels came through the youth system with Bayern, and made one senior appearance for them until being sold to Dortmund in 2009. Seven years later Bayern paid £30 million to bring him back to Munich. He returned to Dortmund again in 2019.

Mario Gotze

The man who scored the winning goal in the 2014 FIFA World Cup final, Gotze is another man to complete the move each way. In 2013, Bayern paid Dortmund £40 million for his services, only to sell him back for a little more than half of that, three years later.

Niklas Süle

The most recent man to make the switch, German international defender Süle has just joined Dortmund on a free transfer following the expiry of his contract with Bayern.

Interesting facts about the rivalry

- The two clubs have the highest average attendance in Europe.
- The very first meeting between the two in the Bundesliga was as recently as 1965, Dortmund won 2 – 1 and Franz Beckenbauer missed a penalty for Bayern.
- Although the two have become rivals in recent years, both clubs have local teams that they consider their more traditional rivals. In the case of Dortmund it is Schalke, whilst for Bayern it is fellow Bavarians Nürnberg.
- Der Klassiker is a generic term in German for any match between leading teams. In fact, it was originally used to describe games between Bayern and Borussia Mönchengladbach when they were one of the dominant forces in German football, and it has only been since the rise of Dortmund it has gained its recent connotation.

THE SECOND CITY DERBY

ASTON VILLA V BIRMINGHAM CITY

Location: Black Country, England

First Meeting: 2 January 1886

The Birmingham derby is arguably the fiercest of rivalries in the teams from West Midlands, although matches between the two involving West Bromwich Albion and Wolverhampton Wanderers also have a claim as well.

The name the Black Country, where these two clubs are located, owes its origins to the mid-nineteenth century when the region was home to thousands of ironworking foundries and forges, as well as coal-mining which blackened the sky with smoke and obnoxious fumes.

Much of that industry is now gone, lost to cheaper third world countries, but the name remains as a legacy.

In brief, Aston was once a parish in Warwickshire that became absorbed into Birmingham as the city expanded its limits during the Industrial Revolution.

The origins of the rivalry

In the late 19th century, both teams represented townships. Aston Villa represented Aston and the area of Perry Bar, whilst City, known at that time as Small Heath Alliance, represented Small Heath and the growing city of Birmingham.

Over time, as Birmingham grew in size, both areas – and teams – were absorbed into the metropolitan city.

Aston Villa helped found the inaugural First Division, whilst Birmingham began life in the lower leagues. For much of the first part of their mutual existence, Villa fans did not think of Birmingham as serious rivals, taking another local club, West Bromwich Albion much more seriously.

However, once the two clubs enjoyed a spell in the top flight together, the enmity and antagonism grew, and, although they are once again in separate divisions, the rivalry remains fierce.

In terms of who follows which club, there are no clear social, political, economic, or religious divisions to accentuate the differences. Areas that once would have been full of Villa fans in the past are likely to have a strong contingent of City support now, and vice versa. Except for the areas surrounding the two stadiums, Villa Park, and St. Andrews, there is no clear line that can be drawn across the city delineating respective territories.

Birmingham fans are proud that their club bears the name of the city, and sometimes believe that they represent the working class, although there is little evidence to back that up. Villa are proud of their richer history and status, and that can lead to accusations that their fans are self-indulgent and stuck-up.

As is often the case these are just allegations to beat the opposition with, and are not grounded in fact.

Notable incidents

In October 1983, a match at Villa Park attracted headlines for the wrong reasons on and off the pitch.

Before the game even started there had been 80 arrests as rival fans fought running battles outside the ground. Villa scored and tempers back to fray when Birmingham had an equaliser ruled out.

When Aston Villa midfielder Steve McMahon put in a sliding tackle on Kevan Broadhurst which led to the midfielder being stretchered off, things boiled over and continued into half-time, when a contingent of Birmingham players visited the Villa dressing room to continue discussions.

The second half saw no lessening of the tension and there were numerous off the ball incidents. Birmingham then missed a penalty and when McMahon reminded Noel Blake about the score-line, he was rewarded with a head-butt that broke his nose.

After the match, Birmingham invited Villa to continue the pleasantries in the players' lounge, but Villa wisely declined.

In March 2003, a match at Villa Park descended into violence when Dion Dublin and Joey Gudjonsson of Villa were sent off, Dublin for a headbutt on Welsh midfielder Robbie Savage in retaliation for a comment he had made. After the match, both sets of fans clashed, launching missiles at each other and the police who were trying to separate them.

More than 40 people were arrested, and both clubs were ordered to start their next games early. Meanwhile several Villa fans who invaded the pitch were banned for life.

In March 2016, Jack Grealish, then a Villa player, was attacked by a spectator who ran on to the pitch at St. Andrews. Paul Mitchell, the offender, was arrested after he swung an arm in Grealish's face, and blew kisses towards the spectators, before he was led away by stewards.

Most famous matches

Birmingham City 3 – 1 Aston Villa (May 1963)

The two rivals met in the final of the League Cup that year. Birmingham won the first leg at home and then kept Villa to a scoreless draw in the reverse fixture a few days later, to secure their first major trophy.

Aston Villa 7 – 3 Small Heath (September 1895)

If anything illustrated the disparity between the two sides in the early years of the rivalry, it was this match. Villa not only won the match, and the return fixture 4 – 1, but were crowned champions at the end of the season for a second time. Small Heath ended up being relegated.

Birmingham 3 – 0 Aston Villa (December 1982)

In May 1982, Aston Villa enjoyed the greatest night in their history when they beat Bayern Munich in Rotterdam to win the European Cup for the first time. It, therefore gave Birmingham particular satisfaction to bring them right back down to earth with this humiliating derby defeat.

Birmingham City 3 – 0 Aston Villa (September 2002)

This Premier League match is remembered for one of the great comic book own goals of all time. There seemed no danger when Olof Mellberg took a throw in back to his keeper Peter Enckelman, but the Finnish goalkeeper took a giant air kick and allowed the ball to pass him into the net.

Crossing the divide

Apart from the players who have appeared for both clubs, both these clubs at some stage been managed by *Ron Saunders, Steve Bruce,* and *Alex McLeish.*

Saunders' story is particularly interesting. In the 1980 – 81 season, he guided Villa to their first First Division title for 71 years, and the following year they went on to win the European Cup. Saunders, though, had left them by this stage, having left the club in a dispute over his contract. He immediately joined their bitter rivals, primarily motivated by spite. He then spent most of his time disparaging his successor Tony Barton, who guided "his" team to European Cup success.

Interesting facts about the rivalry

- Matches between the pair are often referred to as the Second City derby, because of Birmingham's status as the largest city in England after London.
- One of the most famous incidents in the rivalry involved a match in which Villa did not even feature. In 1995, Birmingham were playing Carlisle in the final of the Auto Windshields Trophy, a competition reserved for League One and Two teams at the time. When Paul Tait scored the winner for Birmingham, he removed his jersey to reveal a T-shirt bearing the slogan "Sh*t on the Villa." He was eventually fined two weeks' wages.
- When the two sides first met at Small Heath's ground in 1879, the Villa players sniffly described their rival's ground as being fit "only for potholing."

Made in the USA
Monee, IL
18 October 2022